Exposé

the search into the secret, shadowy world of psychics and necromancers

by
Mary L. Guy

authorHOUSE®

AuthorHouse™
1663 Liberty Drive, Suite 200
Bloomington, IN 47403
www.authorhouse.com
Phone: 1-800-839-8640

© 2008 Mary L. Guy. All rights reserved.

No part of this book may be reproduced, stored in a retrieval system, or transmitted by any means without the written permission of the author.

First published by AuthorHouse 7/21/2008

ISBN: 978-1-4343-7554-4 (sc)

Library of Congress Control Number: 2008902991

Printed in the United States of America
Bloomington, Indiana

This book is printed on acid-free paper.

DEDICATION

This book is lovingly dedicated to my husband, my friend, Pastor Eugene Guy, for his words from the Holy Spirit as guidance. I must not be remiss and forget my great Bible teacher, Elder Lucius Ford. He was a walking Bible who taught my husband and I. I also dedicate it to my family, for their words of encouragement; Gerise, Gwen, Doug Sr., Minister Johnathan, Wynett, Shalondra, Monty, Deacon and Mrs. W. F. Johnson, my parents and the sunshine of my life, my grandchildren, Kiara, Little Doug, Little Tony, Shania, Andrew, Shayla, and Truss.

I am indebted to my friends, A. Modestine Baker, Emma Smith, and my niece -- Karen Dannyce Guy who pulled this altogether through typing, editing, and suggestions.

May all the blood washed folk find comfort and direction; may the unsaved find salvation.

TABLE OF CONTENTS

FORWARD/PREFACE	ix
CHAPTER ONE *Miss Hattie And Prophet Jedidiah*	1
CHAPTER TWO *Adam, Eve, Satan*	3
CHAPTER THREE *Definitions*	7
CHAPTER FOUR *Divination: The Spirit Of Python*	13
CHAPTER FIVE *A Demoniac And The Deliverer*	25
CHAPTER SIX *Balaam: A Gifted Prostitute*	35
CHAPTER SEVEN *Necromancy*	41
CHAPTER EIGHT *Can The Dead Come Back?*	53

CHAPTER NINE
  Satan: God's Arch Enemy ... 61

CHAPTER TEN
  God: The Only Source Of True Prophecy ... 71

CHAPTER ELEVEN
  When The Dead No Longer Sleep ... 81

CHAPTER TWELVE
  Try The Spirits ... 89

CHAPTER THIRTEEN
  What You Need – God's Got It ... 95

BIBLIOGRAPHY ... 103

FORWARD/PREFACE

I believe that the American society is being duped by the greatest shyster of them all. I also believe that a crime is being perpetrated on us. At the root of this crime is one of the greatest deceptions of all time. This deception is a part of the mystery of iniquity the Apostle Paul wrote to the Thessalonians about -- ***II Thessalonians 2:3-7***. What is this deception? One area of deception is that Psychics and Necromancers are able to help you. This is the area this book will focus on.

Countless thousands are being fooled. But who, you may ask, has duped, deceived and perpetrated a crime on us, the general public? Is it the Psychics? No. The answer goes much deeper, for they are also **deceived**.

Lucifer, the Devil, the Old Serpent, Satan ***(Revelation 12:9)*** is seeking to eat us up. In these last days, the one who is as a roaring lion *[I Peter 5:8]* is walking the airway of American television seeking gullible souls to devour. It is only through the knowledge of God's Word that we are able to identify the works, and the deceptions of our enemy the Devil.

I have therefore, taken pen in hand to record what God Almighty has already stated about this heinous crime.

In these pages we shall ***let God speak***. You will find many scriptures quoted because it is not important what you or I believe about this issue, but the rule of the universe has been plainly stated by our God. Hear ye Him in the following pages.

We must also ask ourselves the question concerning the activity of Physics who are able to tell you things they couldn't possibly know.

How do they do that?
This book is written to answer that question.
Read it prayerfully.
May the eyes of our understanding be enlightened.

[Ephesians 1:18]

CHAPTER ONE
Miss Hattie And Prophet Jedidiah

She lived on the banks of the mighty Mississippi River in one of the many small towns of the grand state of Mississippi. She was in her hey-day, back in the mid-fifties, Miss HATTIE. Everybody knew her. Her reputation as a local "Reader" caused many to seek her for guidance, for deliverance from hex's that had been placed upon folk by their enemies. Miss Hattie's office was her bedroom. She had a large crystal ball, which was filled with what appeared to be water and pebbles. She would shake the ball as the curious sat looking on and then Miss Hattie would seek to know you, your problem and your route to deliverance through a source *other than God.*

"I just help people," she would say, "I don't put hex's on, I just take them off." when you arrived at Miss Hattie's you must not come empty handed. There was no service without pay. There was no deliverance without cash in your hand. She seemed to be a kind, loving soul who was on a mission as her many counterparts in Mississippi and every other state in the Union.

Ever so often Prophet JEDIDIAH would arrive in that same small town. In anticipation, all the residents who had problems would flock to a church in the area two and three days in advance and wait. The pews were hard, yet they sat awaiting the arrival of the deliverer of that day. If you were sick and couldn't get well, if you believed you were losing your mind, if misfortune stalked you on every hand, then get to the reader, get to the prophet. Let them give some dust or a foul tasting liquid and let them tell you what to do. Follow their directions and you would recover. The problem was that when one hex was fixed there was another upon you, so back to the reader or prophet, with more money in hand. It was a vicious circle.

Questions immediately come to mind, why did people flock to these folk, how were they able to tell you so many things that they could not have known, why, how? The questions rage on. In the following pages we shall answer these questions. God has already recorded answers to everything man will face in his lifetime in the Bible. He has given specific instructions in order that we will know which choices to make in life. Journey with me through the Word of God as He exposes the secret, shadowy world of the occult.

CHAPTER TWO
Adam, Eve, Satan

Psychic's are all the rage today, many television stations are raking in massive profits because they sell air time to physics. These psychics are often promoted by famous personalities. It is big business! God's heart grieves as He hears common folk tell of their experiences with psychics. Some expressions are: "The psychic knew things about me that she could not have known." "It seemed as if she was my best friend who had known me all along." "He gave me advice about my future."

Often we dismiss these persons as charlatans or confidence men and women and in many cases that's true, but there are some that operate under the power of familiar spirits. Man should operate under the power of the Holy Spirit; not under the power of an unholy or familiar spirit. Psychics, fortune tellers, clairvoyants, mediums (who are avenues to hear from the dead) have been around for thousands of years according to the Bible's account. God was and is today angry and hates these behaviors. Today God's people are being defiled, contaminated through such close personal contact with the devil and his host of **UNCLEAN** spirits.

There is no new thing under the sun. so let us take a Bible trip back into time to see the origin of sin. Let's go back to Genesis, the beginning. In the Garden of Eden, Satan (which means adversary or enemy of God and man) approached mother Eve to turn her from the leadership of God to himself. Let's go back even farther in time, while Satan's abode was yet in the heavens, before man was created, he declared his evil intent; "I will be like the Most High," *[Isaiah 14:14]*. He did not wish to be opposite of, but like the Most High. He has been a counterfeiter ever since. Satan, the created declared I will be like the Creator. The thing created ought to worship the One who created him.

We trace Lucifer's steps into the Garden of Eden where a serpent surrendered his body to the use of the evil one. Through enticements he sought to control God's man, the one to whom dominion had been given over the earth. He sought to direct the lives of Adam and Eve by appealing to all that was natural or earthbound in them; the lust of their flesh, the lust of their eyes, and their desire to be somebody special in this life. Satan wanted them to forget their contact with heaven. In their quest for these things that Satan offered they lost sight as well as possession of the most important thing - *Life*, and the joyous fulfillment's in the spiritual realm. When Adam and Eve hearkened to the voice of Satan, God's arch enemy, they received *Death* as God had warned them.

Exposé

Let us examine more closely Satan's conversation with the woman and through the woman he influenced the man and through the man the ultimate influence of ***ALL MEN***, in fact, of all ***CREATION***. Keep in focus, however, God's word to the man. *[Genesis 2:16-17]* "And the Lord God commanded the man, saying, Of every tree of the garden thou mayest freely eat: But of the tree of the knowledge of good and evil, thou shall not eat of it: for in the day that thou eatest thereof <u>thou shalt surely die</u>." read ***Genesis 3:1-19***. Now the first question Satan poses,"Yea, hath God said..." Satan damaged himself by seeking self advancement at any cost? "There is a way which seemeth right unto a man, but the end thereof are the ways of death." ***[Proverbs 14:12]***

Eve wanted wisdom and elevation to a higher status. She did not want to receive her blessings through waiting on God but rather they would be as gods, already having their information given through the tree of knowledge of good and evil, a source other than God. This was a leading away of Eve from dependence on God to follow the evil one's plan. Today, even as in Mother Eve's day, when we forsake God's agenda, we are automatically on Satan's agenda. Physics and Necromancers (those who seek after information through the dead) are all attempts at receiving directions without consulting God. It is a direct departure from God. We today resort to wizards (knowing ones), who peep and mutter even as the nation of Israel did. *[Isaiah 8:19]* We have regressed into an age old sin - not a new discovery.

Mother of us all, Eve, hearkened to the voice of Satan, God's adversary and offered the forbidden fruit of the tree of the knowledge of good and evil to father of us all, Adam. Mother Eve was deceived by the Master deceiver. *[I Timothy 2:14]* Adam deliberately disobeyed God. God had given the command to Adam not to eat. Adam had done as he ought by sharing the command with Eve, yet when tempted he chose to disobey God and bring a curse upon all humanity. "Wherefore, as by one man sin entered into the world, and death by sin; and so death passed upon all men, for that all have sinned:" *[Romans 5:12]* Today, even as in the beginning of time, if we hearken to the voice of Satan we are courting destruction.

CHAPTER THREE
Definitions

Let us hear the warnings of God against wizards or psychics and against spiritual mediums who consort with the dead. **Hear the word of the Lord:**

> *9) "When thou art come into the land which the Lord thy God giveth thee, thou shalt not learn to do after the abominations of those nations.*
>
> *10) There shall not be found among you any one that maketh his son or his daughter to pass through the fire, or that useth divination, or an observer of times, or an enchanter, or a witch,*
>
> *11) Or a charmer, or a consulter with familiar spirits, or a wizard or necromancer.*
>
> *12) For all that do these things are an abomination unto the Lord: and because of these abominations the Lord thy God doth drive*

them out from before thee." [Deuteronomy 18:9-12]

You can be certain that there is no new thing under the sun. The barrage of satanic devices that has been loosed on America is phenomenal, yet old as history itself.

We study what caused the Roman Empire, that great imperial worldwide ruler to fall, but we neglect Israel, the Great Spiritual Leader of Nations. We need to study to see what caused her ruin. Israel grew to greatness with a mission to keep alive the knowledge of the one true God. She was taught that the Lord our God, is one Lord. *[Deuteronomy 6:4]* Israel disobeyed the one true God and began to practice the pagan rituals of the former inhabitants of the land. God's judgment fell upon her. She was led away captive out of the land God had given her and placed in other areas by foreign captors to teach her that He alone is God.

America is at this present time under a massive assault from the occult; it was invited in through our ignorance of God's word. We allowed Satan access through Ouija boards, tarot cards, the use of crystal and many other occult paraphernalia. Yes, even those 1-900 telephone numbers we dial to contact our friendly psychic has become a method of contacting Satan; a way to hear a word of information from Lucifer.

Let's examine the meaning of some practices we engage in to ascertain the future or other hidden information.

A. ***Spiritist*** - Is two fold: The wise and knowing divining demon and the clever and cunning medium. One who is skilled in oracular

Exposé

science because the intelligent spirit is in him. It is a super human knowledge of the spirit inhabiting the human body that makes a spiritist medium.

B. ***Oracular*** - Of the nature of, resembling or suggesting an oracle. Giving forth utterances or decisions as if by special inspiration or authority. Uttered as if divinely inspired or infallible.

C. ***Augur*** - To prognosticate. Any soothsayer or prophet. To divine or predict as from omens.

D. ***Soothsayer*** - One who divines, practices divination. To profess to foretell events. A seer. **Greek word:** *Mantenomai* - which is allied to the word *mainomao* - which means to "rave" and *mania,* "fury" displayed by those who were possessed by the evil spirit (represented by the pagan god or goddess) while delivering their oracular messages. The New Testament writers were careful to maintain a distinction between soothsaying (*mantenomai*) and Prophecy or Prophet (*propheterio*). One represented heathenism and the other revealed religion.

E. ***Necromancer*** - (Greek - *darash*) to inquire of the dead.
Necromancer: Magic in general Enchantment: Conjuration. The pretended art of divination through communication with the dead - *the black art*.

F. ***Divination*** - A pagan parallel to Prophesying. Seeking after the will of the gods, in an effort to learn their future action or divine blessing on some proposed future action. The practice might involve offering sacrifices to the deity on an alter. It is believed they conversed with demons. To perceive by intuition or insight; conjecture.

G. ***Wizard*** - A knowing one, a spiritist, a medium.

H. ***Psychics*** - Websters' Collegiate Dictionary states that a psychic is one who is specifically susceptible to influence pertaining to the soul or mind or mental influences as opposed to physical phenomena. It proceeds from some non-physical agency. Extra Sensory Perception (ESP), clairvoyance and telepathy are all associated with this. Then there are those

Exposé

psychics who refer to the spirit that motivates them.

Psychics, fortune telling, readings and divination are synonymous to one another and opposite of prophecy. The difference between them is so graphically explained in the *Imperial Bible Dictionary*.

The difference between prophecy and divination is…that the one is a human device, the other a divine gift. Divination is an unwarranted prying into the future by means of magical arts, superstitious incantations, or natural signs, arbitrarily interpreted; prophecy is a partial disclosed insight into the future by the supernatural aid of Him who sees the end from the beginning. In scripture the diviners were false prophets and divinations were allied to witchcraft and idolatry and energized by demon powers.

Every person who uses a psychic service should ask himself or herself this question - Where do they get their information from?

Divination is a foretelling of future events, or discovering things secret by the aid of superior beings, or other than human means. Divination is condemned because a prying into the future clouds the mind with superstition, and it would be an incentive to idolatry. Now both categories (those who use trickery or those who use demon spirits to read the one who seeks counseling) have one goal - to direct your life. Usually the motive is to make money. Indeed the love of money is the root of all evil! Psychics are not a new addition to our modern culture. It is just simply fortune telling revisited. *[I Timothy 6:10]*

CHAPTER FOUR
Divination: The Spirit Of Python

In *Acts 16:16-40* we read of a young girl who had a spirit of divination. The Greek word (which is the original language of the New Testament), for divination is spirit of Python. In Greek mythology, dwelling at the foot of Mount Parnessus, in Pytho, was a serpent or dragon whose name was Puthin, or in English, Python. He guarded the oracle of Delphi; he was slain by Apollo at which time that name was transferred to Apollo. In actuality Satan is called in the scriptures that old serpent and the dragon. In truth he has not been killed by anybody. However, I am happy to report that Jesus took the keys of death and of hell from the old serpent. We are told by the Apostle Paul: "And having spoiled principalities and powers, he made a shew of them openly, triumphing over them in it." *[Colossians 2:15, Revelation 1:18]*

After Apollo was given the name Python the term divination was applied to diviners or soothsayers who are fortune tellers of events because they were regarded as inspired by the god Apollo. Since Apollo was an idol god and unable to do or be anything (for an idol is nothing): *[I Corinthians 8:4]* then any work of foretelling done by these soothsayers, these psychics, must be demonically inspired.

This young girl in *Acts 16:16*, was possessed by a demonic spirit. "And it came to pass, as we went to prayer, a certain damsel possessed with a spirit of divination (remember this is a spirit of Python) met us, which brought her masters much gain by soothsaying. Satan, if given a place of dwelling, will often reward you by temporarily providing gain; this may come in the form of money, fame or position. In this case people were paying money for hidden information.

> *17) "The same followed Paul and us, and cried saying, these men are the servants of the Most High God, which shew unto us the way of salvation.*
>
> *18) And this did she many days. But Paul, being grieved, turned and said to the spirit, I command thee in the name of Jesus Christ to come out of her. And he came out the same hour." [Acts 16:17-18]*

Here is recorded an incident that lets us see more into the realm of the psychic. It is not said she possessed the spirit of the demon but rather she was possessed, ruled, inhabited by the spirit. He was in control, not her. An alien lived in her and he is indeed from outer space. She made contact with a space creature. I'm not talking about mythical creatures as we observe in television dramas such as Star Trek, nor aliens who live

Exposé

on other worlds, but rather Satan and his cohorts. He is called the prince of the power of the air. *[Ephesians 2:2]* I am not speaking of the spirits of dead folk either. She was inhabited by a demon!

Demons are the rulers of the darkness of this world; they are satanic cohorts. Demons, or as the King James Version says, devils are numerous, thereby, causing many to think that Satan is everywhere present- he is not. He has a large number of demons spread over the face of the inhabited earth making Satan to seem omnipotent. These intelligent, invisible spirits reveal to their host the unknown things of a person. They are evil, they cause destruction and they are in rebellion against God. All things were created by God but He did not cause evil to come into being. Satan was the originator of sin and all those who rebelled and followed Satan are forever doomed - this includes demons.

This demon in the damsel told her things she could not have known. It was as if she had been a long time friend of the Apostle Paul and his missionary team. In reality she did not know Paul or his associates. She only met them upon their arrival and right away the demon began to speak. "These men are the servants of the Most High God which shew unto us the way of salvation." no doubt the people of Ephesus responded with amazement at the skill, the wisdom of this young woman.

She spoke truth. They indeed were the servants of the Most-High God. They were there to shew unto them the way of life. They were truly men who preached salvation. This young woman spoke the truth! All psychics do not speak truth. Many possess intuition and are skilled at interpreting body language. Some are attentive listeners and can tell you some things because you have told them. Some just know by your age and gender what things might interest you. The Lord says that these folks "peep and mutter." to peep is to chatter, to mutter is to meditate. In other words, they think it through and then they speak.

This young woman followed the missionaries for many days, repeatedly telling all in earshot of their position and their purpose. Their purpose: They show unto us the way of salvation. Her foretelling was elevating the works of Satan, this grieved Paul. Finally, he turned and spoke to the spirit, "I command thee in the name of Jesus Christ to come out of her." demons were created by Jesus and are subject to Him. *[St. Luke 10:17]* Jesus passed this authority on to His children, and Paul, who was one of His children, used the marvelous name of Jesus to release this one who was captive to a fortune telling demon. "Come out of her." Instantly deliverance came, and came the same hour. The power of our God is awesome. The deliverance was so total until she could no longer foretell anything. When the spirit of divination went out of her so did that which some had counted as giftedness - the ability to speak of hidden things.

Then Miss Psychic discovered that she was liked and followed, not because of who she was but rather for her ability. The crowds left her. Her admirers went away disappointed. She was alone. Her masters became enraged with Paul and his entourage because they could no longer use her to make money for them. They had no care or concern for this girl other than what she could do for them. That's so sad. **Hear the word of the Lord:**

"Regard not them that have familiar spirits, neither seek after wizards, to be defiled by them: I am the Lord your God." [Leviticus 19:31]

Folk possessed by familiar spirits are not to be regarded. We are told not to pay any attention to them, even when they have told you the truth. My brother, years ago said, "The best lie is one mixed with some truth; for people will swallow the lie along with the truth." that statement seems so appropriate when one is dealing with psychics. Don't seek after wizards. Wizards are "knowing ones." the reason we are not to regard nor seek after them is because we become defiled by contact with these unclean spirits. It is a known fact that we absorb from those with whom we associate. If your companion is an unclean demon, you also will become unclean. Contact with demons is forbidden primarily because we are consorting with the enemy. Those who are ruled by demons will temporarily gain prominence, but in the end they'll receive what the devil and his angels receive - the lake that burns with fire and brimstone or sulfur. Well, what about those who say "I love God?" then they must forsake those with familiar spirits for they are a bunch in opposition to the word of God. **Hear the word of the Lord.**

"And the soul that turneth after such as have familiar spirits, and after wizards, to go a whoring after them, I will even set My face against that soul, and will cut him off from among his people." [Leviticus 20:6]

To follow anybody other than God is idolatry. How dare we "turn after" one other than the Omniscient One, the all knowing One. God wants to be our Father. God calls it whoredom when His people become enticed and heed the call of a voice other than His own. Jesus declared that His sheep hear His voice and a stranger they will not follow. God also fairly shouts a warning. "I will even set my face against that soul, and will cut him off from among his people." God says I will become your enemy. I will take your very life away. Often when one seeks out a psychic it is in regard to relationships. We are fearful of not having someone to love us. We become impatient with the way our love life is going and we become filled with questions.

I need a husband/wife. What do you see in my future? Is this the right man or woman for me? Should I leave this one and look for another? God says, if we turn after wizards or knowing ones, the relationships we desire will not prosper for "I will cut him off from among his people." he speaks here of death.

God's warnings are pointed, His pleadings are even more so. "I am the Lord your God…" *[Isaiah 43:3]* I am Jehovah, the self existent One, the great eternal I Am. *[Exodus 3:13-14]* As the great I Am, I will supply all your needs according to my riches in glory. *[Philippians 4:19]* I Am your God. I Am your Elohim. I Am the strong One. I Am the faithful One. I keep my promises. I Am the Lord your God." Such an outpouring of love for His creation deserves a positive response. "I Am the Lord your God."

At this point you must ask yourself the most important question you will ever ask - is the Lord my

God? Church membership does not mean the Lord is your God. Doing good deeds, giving money, being nice does not mean the Lord is your God. He becomes your God only when you believe on the Lord Jesus Christ. He is not your God if Buddha, Allah or as Pantheist say, every thing is God (grass, water, trees) is the one you worship. **Hear the word of the Lord:**

"Neither is there salvation in any other: for there is none other name under heaven given among men, whereby we must be saved." [Acts 4:12]

Jesus is the only name whereby we are saved.

Apostle Paul, when asked what must I do to be saved, replied, believe on the Lord Jesus Christ, and thou shalt be saved and thy house. *[Acts 16:30-31]* That's just wonderful! Through faith in Jesus we are saved, and it can be household salvation. When one person in a family is saved often others will accept Christ as they see their family members faith manifested in a changed life. Why not take Christ as Savior today?

"For by grace are ye save through faith; and that not of yourselves: it is the gift of God." [Ephesians 2:8]

Grace is the love and unmerited favor extended from God to man. It is an unearned, enabling from God, a power from God to accomplish the will of God concerning you. It is this grace that leads us to repentance and thereby to salvation. Jesus Christ is the manifestation of grace for indeed grace and truth came by Jesus Christ. Surely we are saved by grace for even the faith that we possess is from God. "...According as God hath dealt to every man the measure of faith." *[Romans 12:3]* God has dealt or given out by portion the measure of faith to each one and then He has power-packed His words with faith. "So then faith cometh by hearing, and hearing by the word of God." *[Romans 10:17]* God's word brings faith. <u>*To increase your faith, increase your word intake!*</u> **In essence, God is saying, that it is:**

> *"Not by works of righteous which we have done, but according to His mercy He saved us, by the washing of regeneration, and renewing of the Holy Ghost: which he shed on us abundantly through Jesus Christ our Savior: that being justified by His grace, we should be made heirs according to the hope of eternal life." [Titus 3:5-7]*

This salvation is not of works, lest any man should boast. *[Ephesians 2:9]* Some folk say faith in Christ is too simple; surely, it must of necessity be more complicated. Well you're wrong! You're wrong because that is all that is required for a man to be saved:

> *"That if thou shalt confess with thy mouth, the Lord Jesus, and shalt believe in thine heart that God hath raised Him from the dead, THOU SHALT BE SAVED. For with the heart man believeth unto righteousness; and with the mouth confession is made unto salvation." [Romans 10:9-10]*

Salvation on man's part is simple - a look at Jesus through God's word, a turning from evil and receiving God's provision for your sins - Jesus Christ. Now on God's part it was extremely difficult, (so you were right)

Exposé

for He had to leave heaven in the person of His Son and tabernacle *in flesh* with Mary. Since He was the express image of His Father God we could see what God's desire was for man and He manifested God's love in the most awesome way. He died on Calvary! He paid the sin debt *we* owed. Now through simple faith in what Jesus did, we are saved. Thanks be unto God for His unspeakable gift - Jesus Christ who gives eternal, endless life.

Have you confessed with your mouth the Lord Jesus and believed in your heart that God has raised Him from the dead? If not bow you head right now and contact heaven. Confess your faith in Jesus to Jesus through the channel of prayer. Remember procrastinators tend to be lost !!! Pray this prayer if you have believed on Jesus as Lord.

Dear heavenly Father,
I have believed on Jesus that He did die in my place to pay for all of my sins. I believe that He arose on the third day. I am sorry for all those wrong things I have done in my life. Please forgive me. I want you, Jesus, to live in me and guide my life. I thank you now for my salvation. Amen.

Salvation is yours right now! Salvation means to be delivered. You have been delivered out of the ruler-ship of the prince of darkness, Satan; you have been translated into the kingdom of His dear Son. *[Colossians 1:13]* In other words you belong to Jesus. The Lord is Your God - Oh Happy Day, The Day of Deliverance!

Hear the word of the Lord:

"And when they shall say unto you, Seek unto them that have familiar spirits, and unto wizards that peep and mutter: Should not a people seek unto their God? For the living to the dead." [Isaiah 8:19]

How poignant is the plea of Jehovah to His people and it is a question that yet rings down to our present generation. Should not a people seek unto their God? Shouldn't they seek the One who is strong, self existent and faithful, the One who has provided for man, the work of His fingers? Are we not as mother Eve back in the garden? When we look at what God has done we can say with her, yes, God has been good to me. Yet in the next breath we say, but there is more I want to know. We disobey our God and seek unto inferior creatures - man and the demon that moves the man. We are fast becoming a nation of idol worshippers - we worship the sun. In summertime we forget church and God and we follow the call of the sun - to beaches, parks, backyard cookouts, camping. We follow anywhere but to God's house and because we fail to go where God's word is being taught, we are led away by false doctrines. Doctrines of the devil *[I Timothy 4:1]* that:

1. I can worship at home as good as I can at church.

2. It doesn't matter because God knows my heart.

3. God knows I don't have but two days off and I want to spend it with my family.

4. I get tired of those hot, tight clothes you have to wear to church.

Exposé

Excuses, all of these are excuses. God said He had prepared a feast and He had given an invitation to <u>all</u> the world to come and dine with Him. With one consent they began to make excuses. These excuses so angered the Lord that He declared, in ***St. Luke 14:24:*** "...None of those men which were bidden (invited) shall taste of My supper." many folk are mistakenly believing that they shall eat bread in the kingdom of God but do not realize they have rendered their invitation non-effectual because of their excuses. Just think about it, when a man loves a woman, or vice versa, they want some of that loved one's time. God wants our time, our respect, our commitment, our dedication and most of all He wants our surrender to His will for our lives. We are idolaters, whether we worship the sun or the moon, psychics, necromancers, family or mate. God is a jealous God. ***[Exodus 34:14]***

CHAPTER FIVE
A Demoniac And The Deliverer

St. Mark 5:1-20 reads:
1. And they came over unto the other side of the sea, into the country of the Gadarenes.

2. And when he was come out of the ship, immediately there met him out of the tombs a man with an unclean spirit,

3. Who had his dwelling among the tombs; and no man could bind him, no, not with chains:

4. Because that he had been often bound with fetters and chains, and the chains had been plucked asunder by him, and the fetters broken in pieces: neither could any man tame him.

5. And always, night and day, he was in the mountains, and in the tombs, crying, and cutting himself with stones.

6. But when he saw Jesus afar off, he ran and worshipped him,

7. And cried with a loud voice, and said, What have I to do with thee, Jesus, thou Son of the Most High God? I adjure thee by God, that thou torment me not.

8. For he said unto him, *Come out of the man, thou unclean spirit.*

9. And he asked him, *What is thy name?* And he answered saying, My name is Legion: for we are many.

10. And he besought him much that he would not send them away out of the country.

11. Now there was there nigh unto the mountain a herd of swine feeding.

12. And all the devils besought him, saying, Send us into the swine, that we may enter into them.

13. And forthwith Jesus gave them leave. And the unclean spirits went out, and entered into the swine: and the herd ran violently down a steep place into the sea, (they were about two thousand;) and were choked in the sea.

14. And they that fed the swine fled, and told it in the city, and in the country. And they went out to see what it was that was done.

15. And they come to Jesus, and see him that was possess with the devil, and had the

Exposé

legion, sitting and clothed, and in his right mind: and they were afraid.

16. And they that saw it told them how it befell to him that was possessed with the devil, and also concerning the swine.

17. And they began to pray him to depart out of their coasts.

18. And when he was come into the ship, he that had been possessed with the devil prayed him that he might be with him.

19. Howbeit Jesus suffered him not, but saith unto him, *Go home to thy friends, and tell them how great things the Lord hath done for thee, and hath had compassion on thee.*

20. And he departed, and began to publish in Decapolis how great things Jesus had done for him: and all men did marvel.

Before we go any further, let us see, is there hope for the one possessed by the spirit of Python which is the spirit of fortune telling. Yes, emphatically yes! In Philippi, when Paul cast out the demon, that young woman was no longer captive to the demon. She was free but she needed to come and receive Jesus as her Savior. We don't read in the book of Acts any account that she ever did that. She might have spent the remainder of her life grousing, complaining about how they took away her glory days. We don't know. We do know that demon possessed and demon influenced, and demon oppressed people can be set free.

The gospels recount this fact over and over. In fact in *St. Luke 4:18* Jesus declared that He was anointed to preach deliverance to the captive. That was a vital part of His mission here on earth. He demonstrated that anointing many times but none more graphically than in *St. Mark 5:1-20*. Here Jesus made a special trip to Gadara and performed one miracle, the deliverance of a demon possessed man. We aren't given his name, only his condition. He was a man nearing, no doubt, the end of his life, not because of age but because of the demon infestation. It was not just one demon who lived in him but a legion. Today he would have been diagnosed as multiple personalities. Indeed this was the case, for there was a networking of spirits inside this one man. Each demon wanting his turn at manifestation to do that which pleased him. Demons want a human body so they can act out their desires. They drove this poor man mad. He couldn't stay at home or rest in his bed because there was too much going on in his head and body. He fled to the graveyard. The abode of the dead was the only place he was allowed, by Satan, to stay. This demoniac was an example to us. He hated clothes, he lived naked, he cut himself on the stones of the graveyard, he was bloody, he was insane. His strength was immense because of the demons that lived inside of him. When his loved ones tried to restrain him to his house with chains and fetters for his feet, he simply plucked and ripped them off with his fingers. This was a tormented man. You can almost see the demented look in his eyes. This was a maniac!

16) "God so loved the world that he gave his only begotten Son that whosoever (that includes this unlovely manic) believeth in him should not perish but have everlasting life.

Exposé

17) For God sent not his Son into the world to condemn the world, but that the world through Him might be saved." [St. John 3:16-17]

Glory to God, that's good news! Yes, God sent His Son into the world, to deliver mankind from their own self imposed mess. But Jesus here is faced with a man who is unable to believe, for these networking spirits are bombarding him. "Always, night and day, he was in the mountains and in the tombs crying and cutting himself with stones." The man's concerns were the demons concern for he was no longer in control, his personality was so meshed with the demons; they spoke as one voice (the spirits spoke through his vocal chords). Let's observe their behavior upon seeing Jesus:

1. *<u>The demons worshipped Jesus:</u>*
    The man motivated by the demons ran and worshipped Him. Why would demons worship Jesus? Their behavior may sound strange until we read that at the name of Jesus every knee must bow and every tongue confess that Jesus is Lord. This includes demon's and men. *[Philippians 2:10-11]*

2. *<u>Demons imparted knowledge this man did not know:</u>*
    The man knew who Jesus was because the demons knew. We can't help but recall the young woman of *Acts* the *16th* chapter. This demoniac was as all fortune tellers and wizards - they had a knowing beyond human knowledge. The demons know what

many men do not know. They know Him to be the virgin born Son of the Most High God. Notice, they don't call God an high God, but rather the Most High God. In spite of all who seek to replace or to be God, they fail- for there is only one true God. He is the Most High God, and demons in hell tremble at His name - Jesus!

3. *<u>The demons knew Jesus did not fellowship with them:</u>*

"What have I to do with thee, Jesus?" Satan had no part with Jesus. Hear the words of Jesus, **"*for the prince of this world cometh, and hath nothing in me.*"** *[St John 14:30]* Our prayer should be - I would be like Jesus.

4. *<u>Demons were fearful of the power of Jesus:</u>*

He tried to get Jesus to swear that He would not torment them. **"*I adjure thee by God, that thou torment me not.*"** There was an entire legion of demons present and yet they were terrified of Jesus. Why do believers stand in fear of demon power when Jesus has power over any demon? Jesus is the Creator of Lucifer - **"*all things were made by Him, and without Him was not anything made that was made.*** *[St. John 1:3]* He made him, but He did not create him evil. Jesus completed mans triumph over Satan as He died on the cross, **"*having spoiled principalities and powers, he made a shew of them openly triumphing over them in it.***

[Colossians 2:14-15] Triumph and victory over all the works of the devil is a "done deal."

5. <u>*When Jesus spoke demons answered:*</u>

"*What is thy name*" Jesus asked? "*My name is Legion for we are many,*" replied the demon. *[St. Mark 5:9]*

6. <u>*When Jesus spoke they obeyed:*</u>

"***Come out of the man, thou unclean spirit,***" said the master of the universe. The demons began to plead with Jesus. "***And he besought Him much that He would not send them away out of the country.***" And all the devils besought Him saying, "***Send us into the swine, that we may enter into them. [St. Mark 5:10,12]*** These demons did not wish to be without a body. We are told by Jesus, "***when the unclean spirit is gone out of a man, he walketh through dry places, seeking rest and findeth none***" *[St. Matthew 12:43]* This is the state of a spirit who has been cast out of a living host; he walks, he travels in waterless places, he desires, nay, he requires rest but he finds none. This legion of spirits, this network of evilness seeks another live body, for they needed to fulfill their evil purpose. Their plan, to cause this mans life to cease, was thwarted by Jesus. "***Come out of the man, thou unclean spirit.***" Satan lost the soul he thought he had and once and for all mankind can see his evil intent to all. "***Send*** *us into the swine."* Shows us the needy side of demons. They need a body. They need to kill, steal and destroy. Jesus provided a massive object lesson for all of humanity . In the country of the Gadarenes near the mountain, there was a herd of swine (pigs/hogs) feeding. Jesus gave them permission to go, as they had requested Him, into the swine. The unclean spirits went out and entered into the swine. *[St. Mark 5:13]*

7. ***Demon possession caused violence and suicide:***
"And the herd ran violently down a steep place into the sea." It was approximately 2,000 hogs. *"...And were choked in the sea [St. Mark 5:13].* These hogs, who did not have free choice as man did, and did not have a brain that could think rationally, didn't know what to do when assaulted by indwelling demons. They were driven mad instantly. They became obsessed with the desire to rush into the sea. Madly they rushed, pushed and shoved their way to destruction. They were destroyed by mass suicide caused by demon infestation. Their dirty work of destruction completed, these demons, who can not die, begin their search again for a body to inhabit.

Wait just a moment! We dare not leave this Bible account until we know what has become of the host for these devils. What about the maniac of Gadara? What of the man out of whom went the legion of devils? *"And*

Exposé

they come to Jesus and see him that was possessed with the devil, and had the legion sitting, clothed and in his right mind." [St. Mark 5:15] He who could find no rest because of restless demons, he who could not lay in his bed, nor stay in his house, he who couldn't have successful relationships with parents, children, mates or neighbors, he was sitting clothed. He was no longer naked and bloody for he was sitting clothed. He was no longer alone. He had his right mind. Jesus gave him a sound mind: *"For God hath not given us the spirit of fear: but of power, and of love, and of a sound mind." [II Timothy 1:7]*

CHAPTER SIX
Balaam: A Gifted Prostitute

Let us consider one other category of those who "know"- the prophet Jedidiah's of this world. They hear God, our Savior, and yet they are not totally convinced that God's way is the best way.

Name: Balaam

Position: Seer, hired prophet, soothsayer

Nationality: Midianite

Name Meaning: A pilgrim/or lord of the people

This man's story covers **Numbers** chapters **22, 23, 24** and **25.** By his own account he was a man with his "eyes open," in other words, he saw what others couldn't see. *[Numbers 24:15]* Yet this man prostituted his gift. God in mercy confronts this man. God must severely warn this man to speak only what God speaks to him. He hears God, yet he may or may not say what God tells him. There are many people who can hear Jesus but just will not live the life that He requires for His people. This is utter confusion. They can hear the voice of God but will not follow His teachings. This is error; this is sin. People like Balaam enjoy notoriety, even as Miss Hattie and Prophet Jedidiah in that little sleepy town of Mississippi.

Israel, as she marched out of 430 years of slavery from Egypt, encountered Balaam. She knew nothing of Balaam, she was unaware of his existence but in her march to the land God had promised her, she had to go through the land of Moab. She had just conquered the fierce Amorites and Moab was afraid that they would be next. Terrified and distressed the king of Moab, Balak decided they needed some outside help to over throw this nation that covered the face of the earth. So he had a high counsel meeting with his chiefs of staff and sent some of them to see this man whose fame had preceded him. He sent them to the lord of the people - Mr. Balaam, the great one. **Let's examine the message Balak sent Balaam:**

> *6) "Come now therefore I pray thee, curse me this people; they are too mighty for me: peradventure I shall prevail, that we may smite them, and that I may drive them out of the land: for I wot that he whom thou blessest is blessed, and he whom thou cursest is cursed.*
>
> *7) And the elders of Moab and the elders of Midian departed with the rewards of divination in their hand;" [Numbers 22:6-7]*

Now, you must not approach Balaam without the _money_ in your hand. Blessing and cursing people was

Exposé

what he did for a living. He approached God with sacrifices and Jehovah responded. This man was not of the nation of Israel but he knew of Jehovah. He did not know God's laws although he was one of the descendants of the patriarch Abraham's second marriage. After Sarah, his first wife died, Abraham married a woman named Keturah. One of their sons was named Midian. The sons learned of their father Abraham's God. This is apparent for Moses father-in-law, Jethro, was a Midianite priest and he knew Jehovah. *[Genesis 25:1-4]* Balaam knew how to reach Him, but didn't really know Him. This is a picture of many today who hear true things from the true God, but because they don't intimately know the true God they make errors in judgment and in interpreting what they hear. Everyone who hears God must get to know His word intimately to avoid deception.

Balaam heard God the first time He spoke to him about the matter of cursing Israel. God said to Balaam: **"Thou shalt not go with them: thou shalt not curse the people: for they are blessed."** *[Numbers 22:12]* Balaam sent away the elders of Moab and Midian with their rewards in their hands. But the enticement of Balaam was not over, for King Balak sent back a greater reward and carried by even more important persons than before and Balaam, who loved the wages of unrighteous, *[II Peter 2:15]* went a second time, to change the mind of God. *[Numbers 22:15-19]* This time God allowed him to go. God's *direct will*? Don't go at all. God's permissive will allowed it. This man, who could have been a spiritual giant if he had been totally obedient to God, instead goes down in what I call the Bible's

Hall of Infamy - Cain, Jezebel, Korah, Pharoah, Pilate, the angels that sinned and Sodom and Gomorrha just to name a few. Balaam joins this group. All of Christendom is warned do not go in the way, nor error, nor doctrine of Balaam. He is also an example to false prophets and teachers. **Hear the word of the Lord:**

> *1) "But there were false prophets also among the people, even as there shall be false teachers among you, who privily shall bring in damnable heresies, even denying the Lord that brought them and bring upon themselves swift destruction.*
>
> *2) And many shall follow their pernicious ways, by reason of whom the way of truth shall be evil spoken of.*
>
> *3) And through covetousness shall they with feigned words make merchandise of you: whose judgment now of a long time lingered not, and their damnation slumbered not." [II Peter 2:1-3]*
>
> *15) "Which have forsaken the right way, and are gone astray, following the way of Balaam the son of Bosor, who loved the wages of unrighteousness;*
>
> *16) But was rebuked for his iniquity: the dumb ass (donkey) speaking with man's voice forbad the madness of the prophet." [II Peter 2:15-16]*

Balaam's greed for money and prestige caused him to prostitute or hire out his gift. It pushed him to try to

Exposé

change the perfect will of God. God allowed Balaam to go because the man's freedom of choice had bumped heads with the will of God. And God must always allow the man the right to choose. God has set before every man, woman, boy and girl life and death, good and evil; He then pleads, choose life. *[Deuteronomy 30:19]* But it is, after all's said and done, man's choice. This does not mean that God was subject to what Balaam wanted to do. Balaam wanted to curse Israel but God would not hearken to his voice. With God's permissive will Balaam packed up and left to go to Moab with hope of cursing God's folk to obtain the rewards of divination. On the road the angel of the Lord met the prophet and stood in his pathway with a drawn sword. The man whose "eyes were opened" couldn't see the wrathful angel but the donkey upon which he rode could. God gave insight to the animal and eventually gave her a mouth to speak and forbade the prophet of folly, of his madness. Balaam's way was perverse before God and He would have killed Balaam but for the animal getting Balaam out of His way. God then again tells Balaam he must not curse the people. *"Go with the men, but only the word that I shall speak unto thee, that thou shalt speak." [Numbers 22:35]*

After the encounter Balaam only blessed the people as God showed him. This angered Balak. To gain the reward, Balaam taught king Balak to defeat Israel, not with weapons of war, or Voodoo cursing, but rather with deceit. *Revelation 2:14* explains his strategy and *Numbers 24:1-3* records it as it happened. *Revelation 2:14* is a letter written to the church of Pergamos. *"But I have a few things against thee, because thou hast there*

them that hold the doctrine of Balaam, who taught Balac (Greek spelling of Balak) ***to cast a stumbling block before the children of Israel, to eat things sacrificed unto idols, and to commit fornication.***" For Moabs' following the false teachings of the hireling prophet and for Israel succumbing to their fleshly desires, many of them were destroyed.

Many in that day and during this present time follow the pernicious, blood sucking, life destroying ways of the false prophet. When the greed of our own hearts meet the greed of the false prophet we become "merchandise." Our greed may be in many areas even as the prophet Balaam. Some thirst for money, others for fame or power, and yes even for sex but covetousness will always be present when you encounter a false prophet. Covetousness motivates these counterfeit imitations of those God has provided to meet His peoples needs in this area. This covetous spirit allows you to be "used."

A red flag of warning is always thrown up by the Holy Spirit in the believers' spirit whenever anything contrary to God's word is presented to us. If we hear and obey we will not be destroyed, nor used. It is true their damnation is coming but don't be "used" by psychics, witches, wizards, necromancers, fortune tellers or readers whose purpose is to get money from you.

In their effort to use you they are being used by the greatest deceiver of all, Satan.

CHAPTER SEVEN
Necromancy

It is unfortunate that Hollywood and television has used its abilities to glamorize the world of psychics and necromancers. The lights, the spine chilling music, the acting, all depict this shadowy world in a favorable way; although they are portrayed as helpful we must remember God condemns these practices.

There is a dangerous practice being spoken of today on nationwide television. An individual goes into a room painted black, sits on a chair and stares into a mirror expecting to see their dearly departed loved one. There are also many who engage in séances. This is when folk gather with a medium or necromancer to hear from the dead. There are others who are so lonely and miss their loved ones so desperately until they wish them back. They say their loved ones spirit continues to visit and share with them. Many believers are convinced that the dead enter this world at will. Some believe they have never left here. There are those who claim to hear the dead and there are those through whom supposedly the dead speak. According to those who practice this, there are often supernatural manifestations of the presence of the departed one. Sometimes one may levitate (to rise or float in the air by some alleged supernatural power that overcomes gravity - Websters Collegiate Dictionary) or articles may move around in the room of the séance. Those who desire to keep alive the communication lines between themselves and the deceased think they have gone beyond the grave and made that link. This is an understandable practice, for death is so permanent! Death is a painful experience for those left behind. Many die in the prime of life and we would like to have enjoyed their company. Often the deceased was our confidant, our guide and we feel as if we are floundering about in life. We need the stability of that persons advice and so we seek out the dead for direction. Sometimes our loved ones died tragically or in an unexplained way and our not knowing drives us to try to reach them.

This passionate desire to contact the other world makes us vulnerable to demon manifestation. Demon spirits who engage in this trickery are called familiar spirits. They are familiar with man for they hang around man waiting to trap him, to influence him and to lead him into hell. They are unseen except the Spirit of God reveals them unto us, or we desire an audience with them. They know things about us for they are around us, unseen yet present.

I know a young man who in order to obtain a winning number in the lottery wrote a letter to the dead and set a glass of water with it. That night demons showed up visible only to his eyes. They talked with him, they gave him out of body experiences, when he went to church they would poke their fingers in his ears to prevent him from hearing the gospel. They gave him mental illness. Indeed they will show up with an invitation and they will remain long after you want them to leave. Run, flee, escape, repent, turn to Jesus Christ who promises freedom to those Satan is holding captive. **Hear the word of the Lord - Jesus is speaking:**

> *"The Spirit of the Lord is upon me, because He hath anointed me to preach the gospel to the poor: He hath sent me to heal the broken hearted, to preach deliverance to the captives, and recovering of sight to the blind, to set at liberty them that are bruised," [St. Luke 4:18]*

Harry Houdini, that great escape artist, who met an early death in 1926, promised his wife that if there was anyway to escape death he would contact her. He has never contacted her. My friends, the dead cannot contact the living. **Hear the word of the Lord:**

> *5) "For the living know that they shall die: but the dead know not anything, neither have they anymore a reward: for the memory of them is forgotten.*
>
> *6) Also their love, and their hatred, and their envy is now perished; neither have they any more a portion for ever in any thing that is done under the sun." [Ecclesiastes 9:5-6]*

When one dies he ceases to function here on the earth. They have no more a portion, forever, in anything that is done under the sun, their emotions of hatred, envy, love cease on earth.

There is no need for the dead to return. All that we seek from the dead our God is willing and able to supply. You need advice? He is all wise; He is the wonderful counselor of *Isaiah 9:6*. You need answers of what happened to your loved one? This can be revealed by the Father *if* He wants you to know. You need a company keeper? You need someone to fellowship with? Make that someone Jesus. **He has promised:**

"I will never leave thee nor forsake thee." [Hebrew 13:5] "I will not leave thee comfortless."

In the book of First Samuel chapter 28, we read the story of an encounter of the first king of Israel, Saul with a medium. We can learn much from this encounter. Saul had commanded all witches to leave Israel or be put to death. His edict was God's command. (Today many of us see no harm in witches. Some believe they are innocent, misguided, or even helpful individuals, but God said He did not permit a witch to live. We know that we as Christians are not to kill witches. God will judge that!)

Let us go back to the scripture story. Saul was accustomed to receiving directions for his life as king by seeking God's answer through the prophet Samuel. Samuel heard God so accurately until Saul had much respect for his words.

There came a day when Saul disobeyed God and God rejected him as His leader. However, Saul would not step down as king and God broke off all communications with him. Matters became worse

Exposé

because Samuel the prophet died. What was Saul to do? He did not know how to lead the nation without divine help; so he made himself another plan-he would contact someone who said they could contact the dead. He made contact with a witch. Today we would call her a medium.

She lived in the village of Endor, plying her craft secretly. Some acquaintance of Saul told him where she lived and he disguised himself and went to seek help at the house of the witch. He states his request, "I pray you divine unto me by the familiar spirit , and bring me him up whom I shall name unto you." She protests that her life is in danger because of the edict of King Saul. Saul says she will not be exposed and prosecuted. He then tells her to bring up Samuel who has been dead for some time now. She begins to make contact with the unseen world. God does not record what she says or does to reach the dead. We do know that when she sees this figure she screams out in fear. Until this moment she did not know that the guest in her house was Saul the king of Israel. The spirit apparently revealed it to her and she became terrified that Saul would put her to death. She had cleverly hidden herself from him from the time of his edict against those with familiar spirits. Now she has been discovered. Saul assures her she will not be punished. He desires her to speak to him of forbidden things. Saul rescinded his own law (which was based upon the word of God) during his time of need. How often we get in trouble with God because we change His words to suit our situation.

Her connection with darkness was so strong until she risked death itself to make contact with this forbidden world. *"Regard not them that have familiar spirits,…to be defiled by them." [Leviticus 19:31]* The word regard here means, don't face them, don't front them, don't look upon them. It was expressly forbidden by Jehovah.

The king asked his medium, what did you see? Her reply, "I saw gods ascending out of the earth." She is indicating that she saw a portal through which the gods have access at will to enter society from the heart of the earth. She identified them as gods - she saw more than one. In spite of her knowing that Jehovah had taught Israel as a first precept that He was the only God, she defiled God and regarded those ascending from the earth as "gods." She disregarded His commandment. *"Thou shalt have no other gods before me." [Exodus 20:3]* This was a woman in total rebellion. She rebelled against God himself. This is revelatory because Satan is and has been for centuries rebellious against God. All who follow him are likewise in a state of contrariness. If you engage in satanic practices you become like Satan - an anarchist. You have no law but your own. You become lawless.

Saul inquires, *"What form is he of?" [I Samuel 28:14]* What does he look like? Saul is aware he is receiving information through a demon and so he sets himself up for hurt. Her reply, *"An old man cometh up; and he is covered with a mantle."* At this word Saul the king bowed himself with his face toward the ground humbling himself in the presence of a familiar spirit.

The unseen form speaks, *"Why hast thou disquieted me, to bring me up? [I Samuel 28:15]* Saul then relates his dilemma:

"I am sore distressed; for the Philistines make war against me, and God is departed from me and answered me no more, neither by prophet, not by dreams: therefore I have called thee, that thou mightest make known unto me what I shall do." [I Samuel 28:15]

The old man in a mantle begins to speak of the judgment that is about to fall upon Saul. God, he says, is going to deliver Israel and her king into the hand of her enemies. Then the old man ends his statement with a devastating word, *"And tomorrow shalt thou and thy sons be with me." [I Samuel 28:19-20]* Upon hearing the death bell tolling for him king Saul lost all composure, falling and groveling on the floor. Tomorrow he will join Samuel in death. His sons will also be in that place. His beloved Israel will be defeated and many will die. Terror gripped him. Saul learned more of the future than he wanted to know!

All things, my friend, are better left to the discretion of God as to the time of disclosure:

5) *"Trust in the Lord with all thine heart: and lean not unto thine own understanding.*

6) *In all thy ways acknowledge him, and he shall direct thy paths." [Proverbs 3:5-6]*

He wants to direct your paths but you must trust him. If we are not to lean unto our own understanding surely we ought not lean on any other man or evil spirits understanding. They are not sweet spirits, they are malevolent, evil, vicious spirits. They are in rebellion against God even as their leader Satan.

> *13) "So Saul died for his transgression which he committed against the Lord, even against the word of the Lord, which he kept not, and also for asking counsel of one that had a familiar spirit, to inquire of it;*
>
> *14) And inquired not of the Lord: therefore he slew him, and turned the kingdom unto David the son of Jesse." [I Chronicles 10:13-14]*

There are many theologians who believe Saul actually met Samuel; there is another group that believe he made contact with an evil spirit. Listen at the words of the woman who saw the form of Samuel. *"I saw gods ascending out of the earth." [I Samuel 28:13]* The woman who was possessed by a familiar spirit saw forms arising from the earth and she calls them gods. The term gods can refer to mankind or demonic forces. In scripture it usually refers to idol gods or demonic spirits.

Is a believer who has died and gone to paradise for his eternal rest at the beck and call of those who are wicked? Those who contact the dead are wicked because they break Gods' command. Must I die knowing at anytime someone may call for me to exit paradise and converse about the mundane issues of life? These are not issues of my life but things that concern others. **Where is the rest God promised?**

> *"There remained therefore a rest to the people of God." [Hebrew 4:9] "…Blessed are the dead which die in the Lord from henceforth; Yea, saith the Spirit, that they may rest from their labors;*

and their works do follow them." [Revelations 14:13]

Why would God allow man to call forth the dead when He has expressly forbidden them to do it? If the dead could come back there would be utter confusion. Deceased moms would attempt to rear their youngsters left behind, deceased husbands would still try to consummate their marriage relationships. The sounds of little happy deceased feet running through the house playing is utter confusion. Just think of murderers who would like to continue invisible killings even as in their lifetime. Hitler would be able to continue his wicked reign. **Listen as Jehovah speaks:**

"And when they shall say unto you, seek unto them that have familiar spirits, and unto wizards that peep and mutter. Should not a people seek unto their God? For the living to the dead?" [Isaiah 8:19]

10) "There shall not be found among you anyone that maketh his son or his daughter pass through the fire, or that useth divination or as an observer of times, or an enchanter, or a witch,

11) Or a charmer, or a consulter with familiar spirits, or a wizard, or a necromancer.

12) For all that do these things are an abomination unto the Lord:" [Deuteronomy 18:10-12]

The Lord here condemns human sacrifice of children (which is child abuse at the maximum), black magic, calling on evil spirits for aid, fortune telling, serpent charming, being a medium or wizard or calling forth the spirits of the dead. Anyone doing this is an object of horror and disgust to the Lord.

Should not a people seek unto their God? Living folk must not seek after the dead. In the 8th chapter of *Isaiah* starting at the *19th* verse, the Living Bible reads:

> *"So why are you trying to find out the future by consulting witches and mediums? Don't listen to their whisperings and mutterings. Can the living find out the future from the dead? Why not ask your God?"*

Today we need to do as the people of Ephesus in the early days of the church. For two years Apostle Paul preached the gospel in that city. *Acts 19:10-12* also verses *18-19* records the miracles that God worked through the Apostle Paul.

> *"And many that believed came, and confessed, and shewed their deeds. Many of them also which used curious arts brought their books together, and burned them before all men: and they counted the price of them, and found fifty thousand pieces of silver."*

This is the mark of true repentance for they burned all traces back to a forbidden life style. They totally turned from their wicked ways. **Hear the word of the Lord:**

Exposé

8) *"If we say that we have no sin, we deceive ourselves, and the truth is not in us.*

9) *If we confess our sins, he is faithful and just to forgive us our sins and to cleanse us from all unrighteousness.*

10) *If we say that we have not sinned, we make him a liar, and his word is not in us." [I John 1:8-10]*

CHAPTER EIGHT
Can The Dead Come Back?
[St. Luke 16:19-31]

Lazarus was a poor man and to complicate matters he was a sick man. His body was covered with sores. He was unable to work and provide for himself so someone, as an act of kindness no doubt, laid Lazarus at the gate of this rich man's house. It was hoped that he could be fed with even the crumbs that fell from the man's table. We are not told this man fed him at all, only that Lazarus lived in hope of getting something to eat to fend off starvation, to build his body up so that he could feel better. The dogs came around and licked his sores.

In the meantime, inside this grand home, where Lazarus lay at the gate looking for all the world like a bag of rags and bones, lived a man whose name is not given (for it has long since been forgotten) but whose lifestyle is recorded for us. He was a rich man. He had all the trappings that went with being rich. His clothing were of fine linen. He was able to wear a color that only rich or royalty wore at that time - **Purple**. He was clothed in only the best. There was never a concern about there being enough. He "fared sumptuously" every day. What was his daily life like? He made merry all the time. He ate sumptuously, he was shining brightly. This Mr. Rich man lived a life of merriment and to all who saw him he shone brightly. He was a star of his day. Many envied him.

Lazarus, laying in the scorching heat or the freezing cold, no doubt wondered why do some have so much and others can hardly eat. Why wouldn't the man have mercy on him and at least give him a morsel of bread? Day after day, back and forth, from his little hovel of a house (if indeed he had a house) in front of the gorgeous mansion in hope for food. This rich man knew Lazarus, perhaps he had thrown something his way from time to time, or perhaps he had put the dogs on him to run him from his gate. It matters not for he was a selfish person. He was concerned with only himself. It matters not anymore, forever.

For this man died without ever caring for hurting humanity. This man, died as he had lived with the philosophy - I've got mine, you get yours the best way you can. He died, and before they could orchestrate this grand, this larger than life funeral, in _hell_, he opened up his eyes. Before the professional mourners, those folk who were paid to come and cry to assure you of a "good" funeral, had shed a tear, he was in hell, in torment. He who had servants at his beck and call now is alone, miserable and in pain that we can't actually visualize, and that never lets up. **Hear the word of the Lord:**

Exposé

"The rich man also died, and was buried; and in hell he lift up his eyes, being in torments...[St. Luke 16:22-23

His Torment came from:
1. *Fire*/flaming fire
2. *Absence* of water/absence of former pleasures
3. *Powerlessness* to fulfill his desires or to change/upgrade his situation
4. *Memory* (not repentance because he still wants Lazarus to serve him)
5. *Fear* of his loved ones coming to this place of torture
6. The *comfort of Lazarus*

Jesus described hell (or in the Greek *Hades*), which is the abode of the dead, as being in two divisions. There was the abode of the wicked and the abode of the righteous. There was a great gulf fixed, impenetrable between the two; Jesus does not speak here of the grave for that is where the body alone resides until resurrection day. Nor does he speak of the lake of fire, that is Gehenna, where hell will one day be deposited.

The abode of the wicked is called hell and the area where the righteous are is called paradise. Before the resurrection of Christ from among the dead both areas were in the lower parts of the earth. *[Ephesians 4:9]* Christ described the place of torment in *Mark 9:43-48* as a land where there is fire that never shall be quenched. It is where the worm or maggot of the wicked dead does not die. Over and over Christ the Creator warns

Mary L. Guy

mankind it is a place **'where their worm dieth not, and the fire is not quenched."**

Definition:

> Worm - (Greek - *skolex)* a worm which preys upon bodies is used metaphorically by the Lord in this passage. The statement signifies the exclusion of the hope of restoration, the punishment being eternal.

See *Isaiah 66:24:*

"And they shall go forth, and look upon the carcasses of the men that have transgressed against me: for their worm shall not die, neither shall their fire be quenched: And they shall be an abhorring unto all flesh."

You know the really sad clincher in this whole scenario is that no man ever had to go there. It was created for the devil and his angels or demons, but all who follow their pernicious, ruinous ways now have a spot reserved for them. **Here the word of the Lord:**

Therefore hell hath enlarged herself, and opened her mouth without measure." [Isaiah 5:14]

Why has hell done this? Answer: To accommodate those who choose to go there.

11) "Woe unto them that rise up early in the morning, that they may follow strong drink; that continue until night, till wine inflame them!

12) And the harp, and the viol, the tabret, the pipe, and wine are in their feasts: but they

Exposé

> *regard not the work of the Lord, neither consider the operation of his hands." [Isaiah 5:11-12]*
>
> *14) "Therefore hell hath enlarged herself…"*
>
> *15) And the mean man shall be brought down, and the mighty man shall be humbled, and the eyes of the lofty shall be humbled." [Isaiah 5:14-15]*

The inhabitants of hell are cursed.

> *"Depart from me, ye cursed, into everlasting fire, prepared for the devil and his angels." [St. Matthew 25:41] This is everlasting punishment!*

This is sorrow multiplied. *[II Samuel 22:6]* There was no escape from this place, for the rich man wanted to go back and communicate with his brothers yet alive on earth, but Abraham informs him that there is no need to go back for the people have Moses and the prophets, folks who will speak the mind of God; and if the living won't hear the prophets they will not hear one who arises from the dead. The rich man desired contact with the world of the living, but he couldn't get out to come back! Lazarus was not coming back either. There is finality when one dies, you still exist - the wicked and the righteous continue but one resides in torment the other in comfort!

Let's consider the one who has comfort. His name is given, which assures us this is more than a parable, as some indicate, for names are never given is the parables of Christ. Lazarus lived a life of pain and suffering.

His life was full of evil events. The rich man died and so did Lazarus. **Hear the word of the Lord:**

> *22) "And it came to pass, that the beggar died, and was carried by the angels into Abraham's bosom: the rich man also died, and was buried;*
>
> *23) And in hell he lift up his eyes, being in torments, and seeth Abraham afar off, and Lazarus in his bosom." [St. Luke 16:22-23]*

Lazarus had an escort at the time of his demise - the holy angels. They carried him to paradise. *[St. Luke 23:43]* They carried him to a place of rest, a place of blessedness. This place is appropriately called Abraham's bosom for he was the father of those who live by faith. It was the abode of those who died in faith - not yet receiving the promise of the Messiah (*Jesus*) to come.

The rich man pleads for what he didn't give while still on earth - mercy.

> *"And he cried and said, Father Abraham, have mercy on me, and send Lazarus, that he may dip the tip of his finger in water, and cool my tongue: for I am tormented in this flame." [St. Luke 16:24]*

Abraham's reply, although it was gentle, cut to the heart of the matter, in essence he said, you are reaping what you have sown.

> *"And beside all this, between us and you there is a great gulf fixed; (it's set fast, it is permanent) so that they which would pass from here to you*

Exposé

cannot: neither can they pass to us, that would come from thence." [St. Luke 16:26]

Jesus informs us through the Patriarch Abraham that there was no exiting from hell to paradise or vice versa. The rich man wanted Lazarus to return and warn his five brothers lest they also come to the place of torment. In hell he realizes too late the mistakes he had made, the wrong choices and the folly of his lifestyle. In hell he becomes missionary minded. He wanted to warn his brothers not to come to the place he was in. Mr. Rich Man was looking for a way back through paradise because he knew there was no escape from his side of hell. This dead man wanted to reach the living with a message desperately but he found out eons ago that there is no way for the living and the dead to talk. They cannot come back. There is no reason for the dead to come back for there is a God who is unaffected by time, space or death. He endures through-out all generations. Any needs the living have, can be met by Him. The dead no longer are allowed to influence this earth.

Abraham summed up God's view of coming back from the dead with messages by saying:

29) "...They have Moses and the prophets: let them hear them."

31) "...If they hear not Moses and the prophets, neither will they be persuaded, though one rose from the dead." [St. Luke 16:29,31]

That's God's final word on the matter. Let the living ***"seek unto their God."*** The smartest man is totally inferior to our God and His wisdom. Turn to the

Lord, consult Him in all your ways, all your activities and businesses and He shall direct your paths. When psychics and mediums or necromancers are "cut off" by God they go into that place of torment. The only way to escape this is by repentance.

CHAPTER NINE
Satan: God's Arch Enemy

We need to take a closer view of the wicked one whose domain we have been studying about. Prophecy was the original plan and it was God's idea. Satan's answer to prophets was psychics, wizards, astrologers and necromancers or mediums. Remember Satan is a counterfeiter. He made this decision to pursue this course of action while yet a resident of heaven.

Yes, there was a time when Satan was a vital part of the heavenly scene. God created him. His name is Lucifer, which means shining one or brightness. He is called in *Isaiah 14:12*, in the KJV, son of the morning, and in the NIV, morning star.

In the book of *Ezekiel* chapter *28* starting at the *12th* verse - *19th* verse, Ezekiel the prophet gives us an account of the before and after of Lucifer's fall from grace.

> *"Thou sealest up the sum, full of wisdom, and perfect in beauty."*

In the street vernacular of today he was "all that." he was full of wisdom and his beauty was perfect. **Read the list of jewels that covered him in verse 13:**

"...Every precious stone was thy covering, the sardius, topaz, and the diamond, the beryl, the onyx, and the jasper, the sapphire, the emerald, and the carbuncle and gold."

God, in love, had created him a bright and sparkling creature. He also had built in musical instruments, tabrets and pipes made music wherever he went. He was gorgeous. He was of the order called cherubim. He was not created wicked.

"You were perfect in all you did from the day you were created until that time when wrong was found in you. Your great wealth filled you with internal turmoil and you sinned. Therefore I cast you out of the mountain of God like a common sinner. Your heart was filled with pride because of all your beauty; you corrupted your wisdom for the sake of your splendor." [Ezekiel 28:15-17]

Notice here he has wisdom but it is corrupt.

This prophecy was directed to the prince of Tyrus *[Ezekiel 28:1-10]*. Here we see another of God's creation succumb to the lure of the evil genius. Tyrus, in the sixth century B. C., was a mighty and terrible nation, she was the excellency of the seas. She traveled to many ports. You could "shop 'til you dropped" in Tyrus for her merchants were from many nations. Spain, Germany, Russia, Middle East and Africa are all listed in Ezekiel's description of Tyrus in chapter 27. The prince of Tyrus became lifted up in pride because of the nation's beauty, their trade and their warriors. The ruler of Tyrus is describe with the same sins as Lucifer:

> *"Son of man, say unto the prince of Tyrus, Thus saith the Lord God; Because thine heart is lifted up, and thou hast said, I am a God, I sit in the seat of God, in the midst of the seas; yet thou art a man, and not God, though thou set thine heart as the heart of God:" [Ezekiel 28:2]*

It is a dangerous thing to sell oneself over to the devil, to follow him, to fall into his sins, for destruction becomes a part of one's future. This prophecy begins with the prince of Tyrus, but it describes the real power behind the throne - Satan, who is called the King of Tyrus. *[Ezekiel 28:12]* We know God leaves this flesh and blood man and deals with the chief evil spirit because God says he has been in the Garden of Eden. That confirms of whom He spake.

Observe Satan's ranting, his corrupted wisdom. **Hear the word of the Lord according to** *Isaiah 14:12-14:*

> *12) "How are thou fallen from heaven, O Lucifer, son of the morning! how art thou cut down to the ground, which didst weaken the nations!*
>
> *13) For thou hast said in thine heart, I will ascend into heaven. I will exalt my throne above the stars of God: I will sit also upon the mount of the congregation, in the sides of the north:*

> **14) *I will ascend above the heights of the clouds;
> I will be like the most High.*"**

We see plainly Satan's desire to do a take over of heaven. He wants to replace God. God is who Satan wants to be. Don't fret yourself saints because the book of ***Revelation*** shows us the ultimate end of man and God's archenemy. First he is cast into a pit and locked up for a thousand years so the saints can have a wonderful honeymoon with the bridegroom ***Jesus***. *[Revelation 20:1-6]*

He will be loosed for a little season during which time he will amass an awesome army (Gog and Magog: this is a designation of Russia and the Prince of Russia.), to seek to overthrow the kingdom Jesus will have set up in Jerusalem. *[Revelation 20:7-9]*

At this time he is confined forever in the lake that burns with fire and sulfur. Allow me to add a personal note here on the effects of burning sulfur. I had an encounter in a chemistry lab many years ago with sulfur. When heated, it gave off a horrific odor. I leaned my head over the experiment and inhaled. One should never inhale sulfur once it has been heated; for it went up my nostrils, down my throat and it felt like a thick blanket had been placed over my air passage. I couldn't get air down. I ran out of the classroom seeking fresh air. Thank God in the hallway I found clean air and in minutes I was back to normal. The experience was terrifying. Years later, I read God's word that the ultimate place of torture for souls in rebellion against God, or those who just don't make time for Him, is a lake that burns with fire and brimstone (which is sulfur). I knew then I must not go to that place for there

Exposé

are no fresh airways there. There is only pain, misery, the devil and his cohorts. They will not be torturing; they will be the tortured, even as their followers are. **Hear the word of the Lord:**

"And the devil that deceived them was cast into the lake of fire and brimstone, where the beast and the false prophet are, and shall be tormented day and night for ever and ever." [Revelation 20:10]

Our study here is concerned with psychics and mediums and their resource person, Satan and his demons.

In summation, we have Satan as an adversary. He is now the prince of the power of the air *[Ephesians 2:2]*, and the prince of this world system. *[St. John 12:31]* As the prince of the power of the air, I believe this is why we see so many strange unexplainable phenomena manifested in the heavens. As the prince of the world system he is the spirit that now works in the children of disobedience - children who love to sin. He is the power behind many governments. These ought to be God's people but they have chosen not to follow God, therefore following Lucifer. It is a spirit, a demon force that is at work in their lives. They are not necessarily demon possessed folk but rather influenced by demons. These are folk who live under the power of their flesh; if it feels good, do it, they say. They are following their fleshly desires and the wickedness that spawns in the mind. The same spirit that moves psychics and necromancers, witches, false prophets, whoremongers and liars, also drives, motivates, propels serial killers.

The god of this world, Jesus said, was a murderer from the beginning. **Hear the word of the Lord:**

> *"Ye are of your father the devil, and the lusts of your father ye will do. He was a murderer from the beginning, and abode not in the truth, because there is no truth in him. When he speaketh a lie, he speaketh of his own: for he is a liar, and the father of it." [St. John 8:44]*

Satan is a deceiver and a liar. In *Revelation 12:9*, it is said of the devil, that he deceiveth the whole world. Through his deception many mighty men and women have fallen. Jezebel, the prince of Tyrus, Adam and Eve, the maniac who lived in Gadara, the young girl who met Apostle Paul with the spirit of divination, Balaam and the woman with the familiar spirit in Endor, were all victims of his deception. He deceives worldwide.

God has provided an expose' of his activities to prevent this deception; it is The BIBLE.

Some perhaps would challenge the thought that Satan deceived these folk; for after all, they made their own choices. They could have just said no. Actually, in the economy of God each creature is held accountable for his or her own acts. A case in point is Adam, Eve and the serpent. Adam followed Satan's plan with the full knowledge that he was disobeying. Eve was beguiled, deceived and fell into sin. The serpent surrendered his body for the use of Satan, but each received punishment for their own deeds. *[Genesis 3:14-19]* God is a fair God. Even though men who

Exposé

are knowingly following evil are deceived they don't really know the full extent of their pain and suffering in the lake of fire, nor the duration of it. Many of them don't believe there is an after life. They are unaware of the hideousness of the "lake that burneth with fire..." They are deceived. There is really no need for this however, because God has recorded in scripture an expose' of the evil one. Man will not take the time to read God's Word; hence they are ***"destroyed for the lack of knowledge" [Hosea 4:6]*** of God's will.

The Anti-Christ, that creature who will act more like a beast than a man, that one who will wreck havoc on society in the end time:

> *9) "Even him, whose coming is after the working of Satan with all power and signs and lying wonders,*
>
> *10) And with all deceivableness of unrighteousness in them that perish," [II Thessalonians 2:9-10]*

He will deceive the whole world, but at the same time he is being deceived. Here is wisdom: <u>Deceivers are deceived.</u>

Many times Satan deceives through the blinding of the minds of his victims.

> *3) "But if our gospel be hid, it is hid to them that are lost:*
>
> *4) In whom the god of this world hath blinded the minds of them which believe not, lest the light of the glorious gospel of Christ, who is*

> *the image of God, should shine unto them."*
> *[II Corinthians 4:3-4]*

Satan blinds the mind of people who don't believe. His purpose in this activity is to cause them to be lost, lost to salvation, lost to eternal life, and lost to fellowship with God. Satan's desire is for you to be lost. If the gospel of Jesus Christ is listened to and believed upon we would not be lost. Faith causes light of this most glorious gospel to shine magnificently upon us.

Is your mind blinded because of unbelief?

Are you aware of how dangerous it is to reject truth? We believe and follow folk who make up lies. Psychics and necromancers tell you lies concerning the after life. They tell you what their demon guides say. Demons want you to believe that it doesn't matter what you believe about Jesus you will still be safe. Everybody goes to a lovely place with bright lights and family. This is a deception. You better check out God's word before you die because if you don't it will be too late to change. Please don't reject the truth. Forsake psychics. Forsake contacting the dead and *LIVE*.

Hear this word, psychics, necromancers, wizards, witches and all who are involved in the occult or who worship Satan: those who follow Lucifer are following a fallen and doomed creature. They are following a liar, a murderer and a thief. Be warned, his purpose is to kill you, steal from you and destroy you. *[St. John 10:10]*

Run, run, run away from him and run into the loving arms of Jesus. He loves you and has redeemed you, but you must receive Him. You must, through an act of your will, choose Jesus as Savior.

Exposé

Hear the plea of the Lord:

"See, I have set before thee this day life and good, and death and evil;" [Deuteronomy 30:15]

"...Therefore choose life, that both thou and thy seed may live:" [Deuteronomy 30:19]

CHAPTER TEN
God: The Only Source Of True Prophecy

> *"For the testimony of Jesus Christ is the spirit of prophecy." [Revelation 19:10]*
>
> *"For the prophecy came not in old times by the will of man, but holy men of God spake as they were moved by the Holy Spirit." [II Peter 1:21]*

John the Apostle, author of the book of **Revelation**, gives us to know that true prophecy will always generate from Jesus Christ. "All scripture is given by inspiration of God." *[II Timothy 3:16]* Much of scripture is prophecy therefore all true prophecy is given by inspiration of God. **Hear God declare:**

> *9) "…For I am God, and there is none else; I am God, and there is none like me,*
>
> *10) Declaring the end from the beginning, and from ancient times the things that are not yet*

> *done, saying, My counsel shall stand, and I will do all my pleasure:*
>
> *11) <u>Calling a ravenous bird</u> from the east, the man that executeth my counsel from a far country: yea, I have spoken it, I will bring it to pass; I have purposed it, I will also do it." [Isaiah 46:9-11]*

God is the only source of true prophecy because:

1. <u>He is all wise</u> - **Jude 25**, "the only wise God our Savior…"

2. <u>He is all powerful</u> - therefore able to execute His counsel, His plans and purpose.

3. <u>He is eternal</u> - He reveals the end from the beginning.

Let us observe this all wise, all powerful and eternal God as He operates in the lives of men.

The ravenous bird here was Cyrus, king of Media Persia, the second world ruler. God called him and anointed him to be world ruler to get His people Israel back to their homeland. Cyrus knew nothing of God but God called him by name approximately 176 years before he grew to prominence as ruler. Israel was privy to hidden information!

Daniel, one of Israel's outstanding prophets, reveals that God is a revealer of secrets. ***"For the secret things belong unto God." [Deuteronomy 29:29]*** Daniel was one of the Royal families of the Israelites who were led into captivity by the Babylonian Empire. He lived in that magnificent city, Babylon which was led in his time by

Exposé

Nebuchadnezzar the king. Nebuchadnezzar did what the more commonly known Caesars of Rome did - he ruled the then known world. There was a glory attached to this kingdom that the Caesars never knew. God described this kingdom as gold and the Roman Empire as the more common element iron. Our modern day Iraq is situated about 55 miles from ancient Babylon, Nebuchadnezzar's home. As a mighty warrior he won much of the territory he controlled through military campaigns, which he personally led. Once situated as Ruler he began to build Babylon. He built magnificent buildings in the worship of his pagan gods and was world renown for his hanging gardens. The ancient Greeks called the gardens one of the Seven Wonders of the world. Daniel lived in this awe inspiring city which was given to idolatry. Yet he maintained his faithfulness to God when many others elected to follow the customs of the land. It was said of Daniel, Shadrach, Meshach and Abednego, his companions in captivity:

"And in all matters of wisdom and understanding, that the king inquired of them, he found them ten times better than all the magicians and astrologers that were in all his realm." [Daniel 1:20]

We are told the reason that these children of God far excelled those users of the black arts in a preceding verse:

"As for these four children, God gave them knowledge and skill in all learning and wisdom. And Daniel had understanding in all visions and dreams." [Daniel 1:17]

Daniel grew from a lad in the court of Nebuchadnezzar the king, who was a great believer in divination. His board of advisor's included magicians, astrologers, sorcerers and the Chaldeans. The Chaldeans were counted as wise men, very learned, scientifically minded persons. It is believed that the magi who followed the star of Messiah to see Jesus when He was born were Chaldeans, who founded the science of astronomy but also practiced astrology. God proved to Nebuchadnezzar, beyond a shadow of doubt that He alone was God.

In ***Daniel*** the *2nd* chapter, the king had a dream that troubled him but when he arose he no longer remembered the dream. He therefore called for the diviners and commanded them to shew him what he had dreamed, for they were the psychics of that day.

"Then spake the Chaldeans to the King in Syriac, O king, live forever; tell thy servants the dream, and we will shew the interpretation." [Daniel 2:4]

8) *"The king answered and said, I know of certainty that ye would gain the time, because ye see the thing is gone from me.*

9) *But if ye will not make known unto me the dream, there is but one decree for you: for ye HAVE PREPARED LYING AND CORRUPT WORDS to speak before me, till the time be changed: therefore tell me the*

> *dream, and I shall know that ye can shew me the interpretation thereof.*
>
> *10) The Chaldeans answered before the king, and said, There is not a man upon the earth that can shew the king's matter." [Daniel 2:8-10]*

Although true words, they infuriated the king and he commanded all the wise men of Babylon to be destroyed. Daniel was counted with the wise men, advisor for the king, because of his godly wisdom. He did not practice the black arts. This gives us an opportunity to see both classes of wise men at work.

When the news reached Daniel he requested additional time and he would show the king the dream and it's interpretation. Daniel prayed and God, who had given Nebuchadnezzar the dream in the first place, revealed the answer. He reappeared in the kings court and when asked if he was able to make known the dream he replied:

> *27) "...The secret which the king hath demanded cannot the wise men, the astrologers, the magicians, the soothsayers, shew unto the king;*
>
> *28) But there is a God in heaven that revealeth secrets, and maketh known to the king Nebuchadnezzar what shall be in the latter days...*
>
> *29) As for thee, O king, thy thoughts came into thy mind upon thy bed, what should come to*

> *pass hereafter: and he that revealeth secrets maketh known to thee what shall come to pass.*
>
> *30) But as for me, this secret is not revealed to me for any wisdom that I have more than any living, but for their sakes that shall make known the interpretation to the king, and that thou mightest know the thoughts of thy heart." [Daniel 2:27-30]*

Read the rest of the chapter, for Daniel revealed the dream and its interpretation, which is still being fulfilled today. Daniel showed Nebuchadnezzar, who was a world ruler, three subsequent kingdoms and those kingdoms rose to prominence in the order that he predicted. Satan, the counterfeiter, is the source of psychics, mediums and fortunetellers. Nebuchadnezzar knew his advisors were liars and clever deceivers who "peep and mutter." This prophecy told of the rise and fall of Media-Persia, Greece and the Roman Empire. The ten (10) toes of the image that *Daniel 2:42* speaks of is an event, which has not yet completed, but believers of Jesus are confident that the ten toes shall fulfill their destiny. God cannot lie. *[Titus 1:2]*

Although there are many amazing prophecies in the Bible the predictions concerning the coming and works of Jesus Christ are wonderfully exact. Let us examine several:

Prophecy: His birth	*Fulfilled*
1. His virgin conception Isaiah 7:14	Matthew 1:23 Luke 1:26-27
2. Emmanuel Son of God Psalms 2:7; Isaiah 9:6	Matthew 1:23
3. Seed of the woman - not man Genesis 3:15	Galatians 4:4
4. Destroyer of the works of Satan Genesis 3:15	I Peter 1:18-20, Matthew 1:21
5. Redeemer (bruising of heel represents His death on Calvary) Genesis 3:15	
6. Seed of Abraham Genesis 22:18	Matthew 1:1, 6,16
7. Seed of David Isaiah 11:1-2	Luke 2:4-7
8. Birth place Micah 5:1-2	Matthew 2:4-6

Prophecy: His Ministry

Deliverance, preaching, healing Isaiah 61:1-2	Luke 4:18,21

Prophecy: His Death

His death by crucifixion

1. Bones not broken
   Psalms 34:20 — John 19:36

2. His cry of anguish
   Psalms 22:1 — Matthew 27:46

3. Piercing of His hands and feet
   Psalms 22:16
   Zechariah 13:6 — John 19:37

4. Stared at
   Psalms 22:17 — Matthew 27:36

5. Disposal of His garments and robe
   Psalms 22:18 — John 19:23-24

6. Why He suffered
   Isaiah 53:5-6, 8, 12 — I Peter 2:24

7. What His death accomplished
   Isaiah 53:10-11 — Hebrews 10:10,12,14

8. Burial suite in rich man's tomb
   Isaiah 53:9 — Matthew 27:57-60

9. Crucifixion with thieves
   Isaiah 53:12 — Mark 15:27-28

10. Vinegar given to drink
    Psalms 69:21 — John 19:28-29

11. The price for His betrayal Zechariah 11:12	Matthew 27:3
12. The blood money used to purchase a Potters Field (burial site for the poor) Zechariah 11:13	Matthew 27:6-7

Prophecy: Resurrection

1. Death swallowed up Isaiah 25:8	I Corinthians 15:51-57 Hebrews 2:14, 15
2. Body would not decay Psalms 16:9-11	Revelation 1:18 Acts 2:25-31 Luke 24:1-8

Are you in need of someone to shape your destiny?
Try the God of the Bible!

CHAPTER ELEVEN
When The Dead No Longer Sleep

Are you aware that God has something spectacular planned for the dead? Necromancers (who are really psychics), say they hear from the dead and that dead people are all around us at any given time, but let us see what really happens when the dead no longer sleep.

Lazarus, the brother of Mary and Martha, of the town of Bethany, became seriously ill. This is not the beggar Lazarus. His sisters sent word to Jesus who was traveling from area to area proclaiming the word of God. Jesus, upon receipt of the notice remained where He was and continued to minister there for two more days. Then He said to His disciples:

"Our friend Lazarus sleepeth, but I go, that I may awake him out of sleep." [St. John 11:1-46]

Jesus spake of Lazarus death. The disciples did not understand this concept that death is but a sleep for the child of God. Throughout the New Testament we see death considered by the apostles and the early church as sleep, once Jesus taught them. He led them and all who were at the home of the dearly departed Lazarus to the burial site. He prayed a prayer of thanksgiving and then He call Lazarus. He whose voice in the book of ***Revelation*** sounds like many waters, called and Lazarus heard. Although he had been dead for four (4) days, and bound with grave clothes, he came out of the tomb alive. Jesus had awakened him and healed him of the sickness that took him into the corridors of death. He had awakened the dead from sleep.

On the day Jesus was crucified, He suffered the awful pains of death, the earth quaked and the rocks rent...:

52) "And the graves were opened; and many bodies of the saints which slept arose,

53) And came out of the graves after his resurrection, and went into the holy city, and appeared unto many." [St. Matthew 27:52-53]

What did this opening of the graves mean? Let us take a closer look. Jesus is called the first fruit of the dead. He was the first to resurrect from the dead on His own. He had power to lay down His life and to take it up again. *[St. John 10:18]*

"But now is Christ risen from the dead, and become the first fruits of them that slept." [I Corinthians 15:20]

Paul explains why Jesus was the first or earliest fruit of the dead in his letter to the Colossians:

16) "For by Him were all things created, that are in heaven, and that are in the earth, visible and invisible, whether they be thrones, or dominions, or principalities, or powers: all things were created by Him, and for Him:

17) And he is before all things, and by him all things consist.

18) And he is the head of the body, the church: who is the beginning, the first born from the dead; THAT IN ALL THINGS HE MIGHT HAVE THE PREEMINENCE." [Colossians 1:16-18]

He is worthy to have the Preeminence, the place of first. We are then told the order of resurrection:

"But every man in his own order: Christ the first fruits; afterwards they that are Christ's at his coming." [I Corinthians 15:23]

When Christ died they buried Him. In the heart of the earth, He took the keys of death and of hell from the one who had the power of death - the devil. *[Hebrews 2:14-15; Revelation 1:18; I Peter 3:18-20]*

He was resurrected from among the dead. When He arose He ascended to heaven:

"When he ascended up on high, he led captivity captive, and gave gifts unto men." [Ephesians 4:8]

When Christ arose, those who had been in captivity, unable to rise again, bound by the rigorous demands of the Mosaic Law, were led out of that bondage and they were now willing captives of Christ Jesus - the long awaited and hoped for Messiah. These all had died in faith not yet receiving the promised Messiah. *[Hebrews 11:13]* Their faith was rewarded when the Messiah, through death, came to them. The graves that opened on the day of crucifixion released the bodies on the first glad Easter morn, for the Christ, the first fruit of them that slept had arisen. These went into the city of Jerusalem and appeared to many in a brief encounter on their way up to the third heaven where they were relocated at a new site: Read *II Corinthians 12:1-4*. It is called paradise. It is situated in the third heaven. It is the place where all believers now go upon falling asleep in Jesus.

> *"We are confident, I say, and willing rather to be absent from the body, and to be present with the Lord." [II Corinthians 5:8]*

These bodies of dead folk who were saints got up from the dead and people saw them. We are not told that they conversed with them but rather they appeared unto many folk. Communication with the dead was forbidden. *[Deuteronomy 18:10-12]*

The dead in Christ and we who yet live and walk by faith have another *prediction* awaiting fulfillment. It is the blessed hope of the church. The resurrection of Christ was the assurance of every believer that He was able to bring this highly anticipated event to pass:

> *13) "But I would not have you to be ignorant, brethren, concerning them which are asleep,*

Exposé

> *that ye sorrow not, even as others which have no hope.*
>
> *14) For if we believe that Jesus died and rose again, even so them also which sleep in Jesus will God bring with him.*
>
> *15) For this we say unto you by the word of the Lord, that we which are alive and remain unto the coming of the Lord shall not prevent them which are asleep.*
>
> *16) For the Lord himself shall descent from heaven with a shout, with the voice of the arch-angel, and with the trump of God: and the dead in Christ shall rise first:*
>
> *17) Then we which are alive and remain shall be caught up together with them in the clouds, to meet the Lord in the air: and so shall we ever be with the Lord.*
>
> *18) Wherefore comfort one another with these words." [I Thessalonians 4:13-18]*

Notice here that the dead do not get up until Jesus returns and gives a shout, the voice of the Archangel will sound and a trumpet will blast. Then and only then will the dead bodies awake and there will be a mass resurrection.

> *51) "Behold, I shew you a mystery: we shall not all sleep, but we shall all be changed,*
>
> *52) In a moment, in the twinkling of an eye, at the last trump: for the trumpet shall sound,*

> *and the dead shall be raised incorruptible, and we shall be changed.*
>
> *53) For this corruptible must put on incorruption, and this mortal must put on immortality."* [I Corinthians 15:51-53]

Here we see that some folks will be alive when he comes and they shall exchange their mortality for immortality. Those who have died and their bodies are corrupt will put on incorruption. Never will believers be subject to death again!

Great king David of the nation of Israel knew the fate of the dead. David sinned with Bathsheba and out of this ungodly relationship was born a child. This child lived for seven days extremely ill, during which time David fasted and prayed. Upon learning of the child's death he arose, went to the house of God and prayed, returned home and ate food. His servants were perplexed because he had been so sad before the child's demise and now he was content. David explained his behavior with words we can all live by:

> *22) "…While the child was yet alive, I fasted and wept: for I said, who can tell whether God will be gracious to me, that the child may live?*
>
> *23) But now he is dead, wherefore should I fast? can I bring him back again? I shall go to him, but he shall not return to me."* [II Samuel 12:22-23]

When we pass from life to death, if we are saved, we shall go where our dearly departed, saved loved ones

Exposé

have gone, but they cannot come back to us. The glad reunion that awaits us is one of the joys of the church. If we are not saved and our loved ones are unsaved we are not told of the fellowship in hell - only misery, pain and suffering. *[St. Mark 9:43-47]*

Yes, there is coming a day when the dead will no longer sleep. Their bodies will arise, some from graves of dirt and clay, others from graves of water, some whose molecules will have been scattered over the face of the earth; it does not matter but all shall rise. Whether it will be a resurrection unto life - life with Christ; or a resurrection unto damnation depends upon the choice you make concerning accepting Jesus as savior and Lord!

> *28) "Marvel not at this: for the hour is coming, in the which all that are in the graves shall hear his voice,*
>
> *29) And they that have done evil, unto the resurrection of damnation." [St. John 5:28-29]*
>
> *"And the sea gave up the dead which were in it; and death and hell delivered up the dead, which were in them: And they were judged every man <u>according to their works</u>." [Revelation 20:13]*

There is coming a day when He shall destroy the most feared one of all time-death. God promises to eradicate, to completely wipe death out.

> *25) "For He must reign, till he hath put all enemies under his feet.*

> *26) The last enemy that shall be destroyed is death." [I Corinthians 15:25-26]*

Our God shall destroy death. Doctors and Scientist have warred for years against this one God calls an enemy, and have never won the battle, although their efforts have been dedicated and tenacious. God, with one move, shall cast death into the lake of fire eternally. No longer will man have to deal with death. Truly God is all-powerful and omnipotent. In fact, the original of our English translation God is El, which in Hebrew means strong one or strength. There is no escaping the omnipotent one.

CHAPTER TWELVE
Try The Spirits

*"**B**eloved, believe not every spirit, but try the spirits whether they are of God: because many false prophets are gone out into the world."* [I John 4:1]

The Apostle Paul reveals that believers will come into contact with those who are possessed with unclean spirits. Believers must not trust every one who says they are of God but test them, prove them. John gives us the acid test, a skillful way to judge the truth:

2) *"Hereby know ye the Spirit of God: Every spirit that confesseth that Jesus Christ is come in the flesh is of God:*

3) *And every spirit that confesseth not that Jesus Christ is come in the flesh is not of God; And this is that spirit of antichrist, whereof ye have heard that it should come; and even now already is it in the world."* [I John 4:2-3]

Only the Holy Spirit of God will give you true revelation of Jesus Christ. He did indeed, according to the scriptures, come in a fleshly body. He always was the Son of God, but since man needed someone to pay the wages of sin and the blood of bulls and goats (which is a reference to the Hebrew practice of blood sacrifice) was insufficient because they were not equal in value to a man. *[Hebrews 10:4]* By one man, Adam, sin entered the human family. One man, Jesus, atoned for sin in the human family. *[Romans 5:15-21]* Through one act of supreme sacrifice He made amends between God and man. It was imperative that a second Adam would come with the purpose of regeneration or recreation.

Demons, who are the spirits John spoke of, do not acknowledge that Jesus Christ, (literally, Savior, the Anointed One, sent by God, or Messiah) is come in the flesh. They deny the hypostatic union of Christ. They deny that He has but one personality with two natures (divine and human) housed in a body of flesh.

> *"...No man speaking by the Spirit of God calleth Jesus accursed: and that no man can say that Jesus is the Lord, but by the Holy Ghost." [I Corinthians 12:3]*

To know who Jesus is requires a divine revelation, the Spirit of God reveals Him. When Jesus questioned His disciples during His earth walk:

> *"Whom do men say that I the Son of Man am?*

Their response showed lack of certainty.

Exposé

"And they said, Some say that thou art John the Baptist: some Elias: and others, Jeremias, or one of the prophets.

He saith unto them, But whom say ye that I am?" *[St. Matthew 16:13-15]*

Here Jesus distinguished between what the world knows of Him and what His beloved disciples would know. Men of the world guess about His identity but His chosen one's, His believers will know. The conversation continues:

16) "And Simon Peter answered and said, Thou art the Christ, the Son of the Living God.

17) And Jesus answered and said unto him, Blessed art thou, Simon Bar-jona: for flesh and blood hath not revealed it unto thee, but my Father which is in heaven." [St. Matthew 16:16-17]

Demons of hell will not acknowledge Jesus has come in the flesh and man doesn't know who He is. It is only when Divinity chooses to uncloak Himself that man knows. Try, test, prove the spirits whether they are of God. God is invisible, Satan is invisible and some folk follow anything that is supernatural. "Beloved, believe not every spirit but try the spirits to see whether they are of God." *[I John 4:1]*

"Now the Spirit speaketh expressly, that in the latter times some shall depart from the faith, giving heed to seducing spirits, and doctrines of devils." [I Timothy 4:1]

Mary L. Guy

When the Spirit speaks expressly one should pay careful attention for this is a matter that will gravely influence the church. We are warned that in the latter days, some folks would be seduced away from the faith of Jesus Christ by spirits. These spirits are extremely clever at appealing to that wickedness that each of us knows and believers have been saved from. These spirits will cause you to fall away from *the faith*. Many yet call themselves Christians but they no longer teach early church doctrine. John the Apostle says they went out from us. This speaks that they went out from among them doctrinally.

These are folk who are led astray by seducing spirits and by *Doctrines of Devils*. Demonic doctrine is there to turn one away from and to nullify the true doctrine. ***Jude*** tells us to earnestly contend for the faith which was once delivered to the saints. This contention is necessary to combat the spirits of seduction who bring doctrines of devils. Psychics and mediums or necromancers seek to seduce you away from faith in Christ alone. Add psychic phenomena to your faith and it will weaken it. Eventually, your faith will become so diluted until you have in its place false teaching or heresy.

Meet a wise man of the first century A.D. called Bar-Jesus. *[Acts 13:6-12]* Apostle Paul met him on one of his missionary journeys in a city named Paphos, which was situated west of Cyprus. This man is called a sorcerer, which here means magician or wise man. This meant he knew things beyond human comprehension. We are also told he is a false prophet. His name meant son of Jesus. Jesus means Savior. Here is a religious man who is calling himself the son of the Savior. He was

Exposé

with the deputy or pro-consul for that country, Sergius Paulus. Sergius desired to hear the gospel and called for Paul and Barnabas to expound the word of God to him. Bar-Jesus or Elymas, which meant sorcerer, for that was his name by interpretation, withstood Paul and Barnabas seeking to turn away the deputy from the word of God. His purpose was to blind him as to what they were saying. Elymas is an example of one working with demon powers. The proof of what side he is on - kingdom of God or the cohorts of Satan- is proven by the stand he took. He withstood the Apostle Paul. Paul was simply presenting the good news of the death, burial and resurrection of Jesus Christ and Elymas or Bar-Jesus made every effort to prevent him from hearing the truth. He was an enemy of Jesus, not a son. He was in total opposition to the kingdom of God having ruler ship in this man's life. He was supporting the doctrine of devils, and if not confronted would have prevented the pro-consul from being saved. God the Holy Ghost filled Paul, and he bound this man's activity with the following words:

10) "...O full of all subtilty and all mischief, thou child of the devil, thou enemy of all righteousness, wilt thou not cease to pervert the right ways of the Lord?

11) And now, behold the hand of the Lord is upon thee, and thou shalt be blind, not seeing the sun for a season. And immediately there fell on him a mist and a darkness; and he went about seeking some to lead him by the hand.

> *12) Then the deputy, when he saw what was done, believed, being astonished at the doctrine of the Lord." [Acts 13:10-12]*

It was astonishing to see God at work.

This blinding was appropriate for he sought to blind Sergius Paulus to the gospel and God blinded him to his surroundings. Remember God's punishments are remedial, that is, they are given to help you to do better. He left the blindness in place for only a season. Beloved, don't believe every spirit for these spirits (and they operate through bodies) seek to turn you away from Christ.

CHAPTER THIRTEEN
What You Need – God's Got It

What you need - God has it. If you need direction - God's got it and He can and will speak to you through His word, dreams, visions, or your spirit. *[Acts 2:17]* When the Apostle Paul was on one of his missionary journeys he thought it was a good idea to go into Asia to preach but he heard a word, a word that it was not possible for men to know. The Holy Ghost forbade them to preach the word in Asia at that time. They attempted to go into Bithynia but the Spirit did not allow it. Then God gave direction through a vision to go into Macedonia. *[Acts 16:6-10)* We do not need psychics and the "dead" to know. God knows and can show you what you need to know. Remember Jesus is God.

> *47) "Jesus saw Nathanael coming to him, and saith of him, Behold an Israelite indeed, in whom is no guile!*
>
> *48) Nathanael saith unto him, Whence knowest thou me? Jesus answered and said unto him,*

> *Before that Philip called thee, when thou wast under the fig tree, I saw thee.*
>
> *49) Nathanael answered and saith unto him, Rabbi, thou are the Son of God; thou art the King of Israel." [St. John 1:47-49]*

God knows the thoughts of men. That which man thinks he does in the privacy of his mind God reads as an open book. "And Jesus knowing their thoughts said…" *[St. Matthew 9:4]*

> *24) "But Jesus did not commit himself unto them, because he knew all men.*
>
> *25) And needed not that any should testify of man: for he knew what was in man." [St. John 2:24-25*

God sees the secret sins in a man's heart.

One day Jesus preached a sermon against covetousness and the Pharisees, who outwardly appeared righteous but inwardly were filled with covetousness began to deride Him. To deride is to turn up the nose at. Jesus quickly identified the reason and that is a sobering fact.

The psalmist David declared:

> *1) "O Lord, thou hast searched me, and known me.*
>
> *2) Thou knowest my downsitting and mine uprising, thou understandest my thought afar off.*
>
> *4) …There is not a word in my tongue, but, lo, O Lord, thou knowest it altogether.*

Exposé

> *6) ...Such knowledge is too wonderful for me; it is high, I cannot attain unto it." [Psalms 139:1-6]*

Man nor demon can attain, or reach the knowledge of God. God will reveal your mate to you if you seek His face in the matter. Now he does this in His own way and at His own time. In ***Genesis 24th*** chapter, Abraham sent his servant back to his own people to pick a bride for Isaac. He depended on God's dispatching an angel to go before his servant. The servant made the long, arduous journey and upon reaching his destination prayed to God to show him the right girl. "Let the same be she that thou hast appointed for thy servant Isaac." *[Genesis 24:14]*

Read the entire chapter. God answered his prayer and revealed the mate for Isaac. Don't resort to wizards that "peep and mutter." Should not a people resort to the Lord their God?

God will deliver you out of the hands of your enemy. In ***II Kings 6:8-17***, we read of the king of Syria holding private strategy meetings to plan the capture of Israel. Every place he agreed to set traps to capture Israel God revealed it to the prophet Elisha. He in turn told the king of Israel of the location. Thus Israel escaped out of his hand. This happened a few times and the king of Syria decided he had a spy on his hand. He called a meeting and inquired:

> *11) "...Will ye not show me which of us is for the king of Israel?*
>
> *12) And one of his servants said, None my Lord, O king: but Elisha, the prophet that is in*

> *Israel, telleth the king of Israel the words that thou speaketh in thy bed chamber."* *[II Kings 6:11-12]*

In some cases God will reveal the personal future of a man, at other times He reveals world wide purpose. Agabus was a man who flowed fluently in the prophetic office during the days of the Apostle Paul. Twice we read of him prophesying. The first prophecy concerned all the world. He arrived in Antioch from Jerusalem with a company of prophets. The Holy Spirit moved upon Agabus and he stood and began to speak as the Spirit gave him utterance, saying, "...that there should be great dearth throughout all the world." This great dearth - time of hunger or want, came upon the earth, according to the scripture record, in the days of Claudius Caesar. *[Acts 11:27-28]* On another occasion Paul and his missionary team were dwelling at Caesarea when Ababus arrived in town. He took Paul's sash and bound his own hands and feet and said: "...Thus saith the Holy Ghost, So shall the Jews at Jerusalem bind the man that owneth this girdle and shall deliver him into the hands of the Gentiles." *[Acts 21:11]*

Upon hearing this his friends tried to persuade him not to go. Paul was determined to go to Jerusalem. He chose to go. Paul was indeed arrested and bound. This prophecy did indeed come to pass. This which seemed to be defeat, however, opened the door to witnessing of such magnitude as he had never experienced before. Through his arrest he fulfilled the prophecy God revealed to Ananias as God told him to go and pray for Paul that he might receive his sight. *[Acts 9:10-12]* Speaking unto Ananias, the Lord said:

Exposé

"...Go thy way: for he is a chosen vessel unto me, to bear my name before the Gentiles, and kings, and the children of Israel." [Acts 9:15]

Paul's arrest and appeals gave him audience before kings, who in hearing this case heard the gospel. Paul's life was indeed so intermeshed with Jesus that he couldn't tell his experience without presenting the death, burial and resurrection of his Savior. Thus, Paul bore the name of Jesus not only to the Gentiles and Israel, but in his suffering and imprisonment he gave witness of that most precious name Jesus, before kings. One can see that God loves all men; whether they are rich or poor, beggars or thieves, paupers or kings. *[St. John 3:16]*

I challenge you to read the Bible for I have given but a few instances of prophecy. The entire Bible is to a large extent prophecy. Much of it has been fulfilled and a serious student of the history of nations past and present could attest to the accuracy of scripture. My purpose here has been to help you realize that God does have an answer for you in things pertaining to you and your future. We have an anointing as born again believers in Jesus, from the Holy One, and because of this anointing we "know all things." *[I John 2:20]* The anointing that abides in us continually gives us insight and wisdom. When we approach the Father in Jesus name this anointing will reveal unto us the things we need at the time we need it. Believers world - wide can testify that He forewarns us of danger, He guides us into all truth, He tells us this is the way to go with our lives. There is now a resident guide *in* the believer - He is God the Holy Ghost. We never have to worry or fret about major decisions because, as believers, we have access to the very throne room of God. That's amazing. We, little insignificant folk, can bow here on earth and reach heaven with no electronic "thing-a-majig." We don't have to shout, scream or yell; we don't even have to say a word out loud, just pour out our hearts, and He who sits on the throne, gives us audience. If I had 10,000 tongues I would praise Him with everyone for the love, the wisdom and the provision of God for His man.

> *"Let us therefore come boldly unto the throne of grace, that we may obtain mercy, and find grace to help in the time of need." [Hebrews 4:16]*

Listen at a description of the work of the anointing: Jesus Christ is speaking:

> *13) "Howbeit when he the Spirit of truth, is come, he will guide you into all truth: for he shall not speak of himself; but whatsoever he shall hear, that shall he speak: and he will shew you things to come.*
>
> *14) He shall glorify me: for he shall receive of mine, and shall shew it unto you." [St. John 16:13-14]*
>
> *But the anointing which ye have received of him abideth in you, and ye need not that any man teach you: but as the same anointing teaches you of all things, and is truth, and is no lie, and even as it hath taught you, ye shall abide in him." [I John 2:27]*

Exposé

Yes, the anointing will shew you things to come, and guide you into all truth because He is the Spirit of Truth - He is God and God cannot lie. *[Titus 1:2]* He is also identified as glorifying Jesus. All spirits do not glorify Jesus. All spirits believe in God. Hear *James 2nd* chapter *19th* verse: *"Thou believest that there is one God, thou doest well: the devils also believe, and tremble."*

There is the Holy Spirit (in the singular) and there are demon spirits (that's plural) and the demons or devils as KJV calls them, believe in God and tremble at him. They are spirits and they can see God, they remember when they were in heaven with Him and the joys they experienced for perhaps eons of time. They remember how they followed Lucifer and the awesome power of an angry God in their being cast out of heaven. Yes, the devils do believe and tremble. They will never worship God, however. You, my friend, are invited to become a part of the family of God, that you might receive all these blessings and benefits.

"Believe on the Lord Jesus Christ and thou shalt be saved. For by grace are ye saved through faith; and that not of yourselves: it is the gift of God: Not of works, lest any man should boast." [Acts 16:31; Ephesians 2:8-9]

Remember, no one is ever worthy of salvation, it is simply by His mercy and His grace that we are saved. Grace is favor shown to us when we didn't deserve it; grace is an enabling power to do all that God desires us to do and to be all that He wants us to be. No, my friend, you can't earn it. You'll never deserve it. All honor goes to God for it. Just simply receive it. Hear the word of the Lord and act on it!

> *"That if thou shalt confess with thy mouth the Lord Jesus, and shalt believe in thine heart that God hath raised him from the dead, thou shalt be saved." [Romans 10:9]*

What should be your response to all these things you have read?

> **Run, don't walk to the nearest exit, away from the occult for that is who and what psychics and necromancers or mediums are.**

RUN INTO THE LOVING, ALL POWERFUL ARMS OF JESUS. HE WILL DELIVER, HE WILL RELEASE ALL WHO ARE HELD CAPTIVE BY SATAN

ATTACH YOURSELF TO AN ASSEMBLY OF BELIEVERS FOR CONTINUED SUPPORT.

St. Luke 4:18
Hebrews 10:25

BIBLIOGRAPHY

We expresses grateful appreciation for information gleamed from the following sources for chapter three (3), on Definitions.

1.Merrill F. Unger, The New Unger's Bible Dictionary, "Cause and effect of captivity," (Chicago,1988)

2. The New Unger's Bible Dictionary, "Spiritist", (Chicago, 1988)

3. Webster's Collegiate Dictionary

4. Vine, Unger, White, Vine's Complete Expository Dictionary, (Nashville, 1985)

5. Robert Young, Young's Analytical Concordance to the Bible, (Michigan, 1991)

6. The New Unger's Bible Dictionary, "Divination"

7. Sir William Smith, Nashville, Nelson, A Dictionary of the Bible, "Divination," (1986)

Printed in the United States
148679LV00001B/14/P